Souvenirs
of a
Childhood Interrupted

by Fred Franklin

Developmental Editing by Vivien Kooper

First published by Dog Ear Publishing
4011 Vincennes Rd
Indianapolis, IN 46268
www.dogearpublishing.net

ISBN: 978-1-4575-3656-4

This book is printed on acid-free paper.

Printed in the United States of America

It was the summer of 1973 and I had given a barbecue that day for a bunch of the guys from the construction job where I worked. I'm talking about killing the hog, cleaning him, cutting and hauling the wood, tending the fire for making coals, and cooking some of the best barbecue you ever ate!

I had done most of the work the day before, but I hadn't begun the actual cooking until early that morning. It was July in Louisiana, and it had taken quite a bit of beer to keep me cooled down while shoveling red-hot coals out of a fire, and then standing over my homemade cooker which was set flat on the ground and looked like a tin coffin. For ten hours straight, I was breathing smoke from my homemade hell, and I'd worked up quite a thirst.

After all that, I still had to make sure everything ran smoothly when everyone showed up, drank a little beer, and ate barbecue and potato salad (prepared by Diane, who almost had a heart attack when I told her we'd need two gallons of the stuff). Once every last one of our guests had gone, I sent my sweet little wife packing toward home, and told her I was going to the beer joint at the Arkansas state line, to "wind down." The truth was, with that amount of energy, I knew there was only one way I was going to wind down, and that was to crash.

When I told her where I was headed, she said, "Come home with me, please!" But my mind was made up.

It was a twenty-five mile drive from Phillips Ferry on the D'Loutre Bayou where the barbecue had been held to the state line bar. That gave me time to think about how dumb it was for me to be doing this, and to wonder how

I would break it to Diane if I found myself in the middle of trouble.

Sometimes on Saturday afternoons when I left home to go to this bar, I would say, "Well, I'm going to the state line to get my ass kicked!"

She would always plead with me as I was walking out the door, and say, "Please, don't start any trouble!"

"I ain't gonna start nothin'," I would say, "but if trouble comes along, I ain't runnin' from it!"

The state line bar was a pretty rough place at times, and there was always the possibility of getting into a scrap. There had been no fights for me there up to this point. But on that particular evening, I was about three sheets to the wind, although you wouldn't have known it to look at me, with my cowboy hat pulled down so low on my forehead I could barely see out from under the brim.

By now, it was eleven o'clock at night and I'd been drinking since seven o'clock in the morning. I had been doing a lot of thinking about my father and our rocky relationship. He always came to my mind when I was drinking. And during this time in my life, I was drinking quite a bit, which meant I was thinking a lot about my relationship with my father. There were so many things I didn't know about him, and just as many things about him that I knew but wished I could forget.

I was sitting in a rickety, straight-backed chair, my left elbow resting on a small table, and my legs extended in front of me with my feet in another chair. I was watching Zane Matthews shoot a game of 8-Ball with some guy named Keith who I had never seen before but was already pretty sure I didn't like. He had come into the bar with Doyle Gray, another guy who got on my nerves.

When Keith started talking about Vietnam and how he'd been shot in the leg by a 'Cong sniper, I started wondering if I'd been too hasty in my judgment of him.

This cat don't look like much, but by God, he's got my admiration, I thought to myself, sizing him up. I had been classified 1-A ever since 1964, but I had never been drafted. There was only one explanation I could come up with—a two-or-three-month period in 1965 when married men were given a deferment and were not to be drafted. It just so happened that Diane and I got married during that time.

We had been planning our wedding for a long time, but during that period, there were people marrying who had been dating for ten years, and others who had only been dating for ten days. I didn't ask Diane to marry me to keep from being drafted, but the fact that it might have appeared that way had always made me feel a little bit guilty around some of my friends who had been drafted. I have always been real patriotic and a part of me wishes I *had* been drafted and served in Vietnam. (And survived, of course! I still have a lot of living I want to do.)

I have deep admiration for anyone who has been to Vietnam. I thought about Paul Johnson, who I knew from school. He won a place in my heart when he joined the army and wound up dying for his country.

I would be distracted momentarily by these thoughts, and by the other people coming into and leaving the pool room portion of the beer joint, but then I would be forced to focus my attention on Keith again. Thanks to his motor mouth, you either listened or you went back into the barroom to get away from him. Before long, he stopped bragging and started berating the U.S. government.

I thought to myself, *I'll kick his ass if he keeps up with that shit!* The guy was of medium build, just a wee bit smaller than me.

While Keith was too busy talking to pay much attention to the game of 8-Ball in progress, Zane was methodically holing his balls each time it was his turn to shoot.

That was Zane, the redheaded wonder. He was lean and rangy and appeared to be slow, but he had the keen eyes and reflexes of a cat.

During high school, he was the only boy who could out-run me in wind sprints. He could also shoot down wood ducks with amazing accuracy. They would come darting through the treetops at dusk as they made their way into Teapot Brake to roost in the shallow black waters that spread out through the cypress and tupelo gum woods there. And with his ragged old pump Winchester with the sawed-off barrel and the electrical tape holding parts of it together, he could drop five quail on a covey rise while I was lucky to get one bird.

Tonight, Zane's shooting was all being done at Keith's expense. Not that there was much at stake; they were only shooting for a beer per game, and Zane seldom had to buy a beer after his first one. Once he got a game going, he would shoot pool until closing time and drink beer off a string of would-be shooters.

When Zane dropped his last striped ball in a side pocket, he simply pointed his cue stick at a corner pocket on the far end of the table, indicating that he intended to make the 8-ball there. Keith was still talking and not paying attention, so he didn't see Zane pointing to indicate his shot. As a matter of fact, he didn't even see Zane shoot and fail to make the 8-ball.

I grinned as Zane tugged at Keith's arm, letting him know that it was his turn to shoot. Keith looked at the pool table with a puzzled look, trying to figure out just where the game stood.

"I missed the 8-ball." Zane caught him up on the action.

"Okay, okay. If that's the way you're gonna play, that's real damned good!" The look on his face and the expression of his words grated on my frazzled, beer-tuned nerves.

"I called the 8-ball!" Zane replied when he realized that Keith was implying that he'd attempted to hole the 8-ball without calling his pocket.

"Bullshit! No, you didn't!" said Keith.

Zane, not easily disturbed, kept his cool. "Well, I didn't say anything, but I pointed at the corner pocket. That's the way we usually do it around here."

"No, you didn't!" Keith just wasn't going to let it rest, so I had no choice but to get into the act.

"Yeah," I said, tipping up my dirty, old straw hat enough to look Keith in the eyes, "he pointed at the corner pocket with his cue stick."

"It ain't none of your business!" Keith seemed to resent the interruption.

"Well," I said, "I'm makin' it some of my damned business!" The next thing I knew, I found myself right in the middle of a fight.

Having managed to get myself ejected from the bar, I was standing directly out from the door with Zane when Keith walked outside with Doyle Gray. Keith had a severe bruise on his left cheek. I smiled in satisfaction at a job well done.

I turned to Zane and said, "Boy, I got a good lick in on him, didn't I?"

"You sure did! He'll be sore for a month. You probably won't see that stranger around here anymore."

We watched Keith and Doyle Gray get into their car and pull out onto the highway, heading north. Wondering, as I had many times, if I might have inherited a little bit of my father's mean streak, I said, "Well, I shouldn't have hit him, I guess, but he sure did make me mad!"

The show was over and suddenly, I felt awfully tired. I slowly walked to my car, opened the door, and got behind the wheel. When I shut the door, I realized how much I smelled like smoke, barbecue and beer. I was grinning as I pulled away from the joint. I was headed down the highway toward the Louisiana state line, but I wasn't really ready to go home yet, and began to think about the night's events.

I knew that, at twenty-eight years of age, I should have been a little bit more mature than to be fighting in a state line beer joint. Reflecting on my behavior at the bar got me to thinking back over my life in general.

As I tried to focus my eyes on the highway at the end of my headlight beams, I felt myself approaching that threshold just on the edge of the twilight zone caused by a combination of prolonged drinking and sheer exhaustion. That course of action had led me to a level of thinking and a particular mood that never came to me any other way. It was a feeling only someone who has been there can imagine. I had felt it before and I would feel it again.

I considered this condition to be a fading of my powers of thought and yet, strangely enough, it was not an unpleasant feeling. It occurred to me that this must be the feeling that keeps driving alcoholics back to the bottle, their subconscious minds leading them there with the promise of a haven of sorts. It scared me to think about the possibility of reaching that point of no return.

I turned off the main highway at Sadie, by the little country store that was also owned by Hoot Gibson, the owner of the beer joint. The road would lead me through Litroe, on down toward Loco and through Dean—backwoods communities between the state line and my old home place.

I thought to myself, *I don't know if I know the way through these damned woods or not! I bet there's people livin' back here in these woods who get lost tryin' to find their way to the main highway!*

I had only been through that neck of the woods once, in 1960, late at night. I was fifteen years old and drunk at the time. Billy Tom Ellis was sitting up front, so I was riding in the back seat of an old Buick—a 1953 model, if my memory serves me correctly. There are two things I remember about that night. The first was hanging my head out the window in the cold rain to throw up. And the second was the driver, Cain Brantley, cussin' that old Buick while it moved along at about five miles per hour in the six-inch deep mud, motor revved wide open, tires spinning, and the engine overheating. It finally ran out of gas in the middle of the road, in the middle of night, in the middle of nowhere!

Cain thought it was funny as hell, but I didn't think it was so funny, nearly freezing my sick butt off before daylight when we had to hit the road and walk about eight miles in the mud to get some help and some gas.

Pulling over to the side of the road and stopping the car, I smiled now, recalling that night. *Boy, what dumb asses we must have been!*

I got out of the car, opened the trunk, fished around in the ice and water in my ice chest for a Schlitz, and popped the top. I slammed the trunk lid and took a long, cool drink before getting back in the car and driving on. As I drove, my mind drifted away from that time, back a long, long way to 1954 and an incident that involved my father and me. Remembering that made me shudder, so I quickly moved further back in time, through my early childhood when life was up and down and 'round and 'round, hanging by a thin line that was subject to unravel at any time, like a worn Yo-Yo string.

My mind raced backward in time, recreating scenes—some as they had been told to me, some as I had witnessed, and others that seemed to rise out of some subconscious cavern of thought. It was there that everything blended together and told the whole story of why I found myself now on this lonely, narrow, dusty road after midnight, easing along at fifteen miles per hour, drinking my beer with no thought of going home just yet, because I still had some things to iron out in my mind.

I drove through Litroe, Loco and Dean, by the old home place and from there to the Ouachita River, parking my car on a bluff beneath oaks laden with Spanish moss and overlooking the water below. Along the way, I had finished three more beers.

The last words my wife, Diane, had said to me that evening came back to me then. "Come home with me, please!"

A tear rolled down my cheek as I thought of how I must make Diane suffer at times like these. The tear was also for my mother, who had said similar words to me way back when. The difference being that my mother had pleaded with me after the violence, and Diane had pleaded with me beforehand.

As morning came, I was still sitting behind the wheel of my car with the ashtray full of butts, the floorboard full of empty beer cans, and the story laid out behind me, stretching from midnight to dawn, a more complete picture than I had ever pieced together before. I had gone back to the real beginning of my story, long before I was born, and in so doing, I came awfully close to answering the question of why I sometimes felt that, of us nine boys, I was the one who was most like my father.

In reflecting back over my life, I discovered inside myself a maturity I had not previously been able to achieve, and with that newfound maturity came an awareness of the need for forgiveness. As the Sunday morning sun shone through the windshield of my car, I thought to myself, *Today is the day I will begin the journey that leads to forgiveness.*

Let me take you now back to the year 1933. That is where my story truly began, for all practical purposes, with my father, Floyd Franklin, and a chain of events that led to an incident that would haunt Floyd throughout his lifetime and, in time, come to haunt me, as well.

One

Grampa had been sitting under the huge walnut tree near the corral since sundown, watching his three field hands steadily plodding along behind their mules. They had been plowing since daybreak, trying to get ahead of the rain. The wind had carried the suggestion of rain the day before, of this Grampa was sure, and now it was only a matter of time before the deluge. He had over forty years of experience in trying to second-guess nature, and prided himself on his weather forecasts.

They had to get the cotton plowed before the rains came. By the time the fields were dry enough to plow again, it would be too late. The cotton would be so tall by then, the mules wouldn't be able to walk between the rows without tearing down the stalks. And the grass and weeds would choke the cotton so badly, there wouldn't be enough cotton to even pay the planting costs.

As the figures of the men and the mules reached the crest of the hill across the field and were silhouetted against the horizon, they seemed to rise up out of the ground. Then they slowly disappeared into the dim light made even dimmer by the far timberline as it rose to meet the hill.

Grampa watched them fade out of sight, his brow wrinkling as he tried to visualize their approximate positions as they continued toward the bottomland to the combination terrace and turnrow. He began to count silently, figuring that it would take no more than ten seconds for the first of them to come back into view. Sure enough, before he reached the count of three, he could see the first mule's head appear above the hill. A smile passed over his face.

Grampa was finally reaping the reward he had coming from putting up with these men for the previous couple of months. They had worked steadily enough through the planting season. But they had also kept the family awake way too many nights, thanks to their drinking bouts and the bickering that seemed to erupt every time they opened a new bottle. The loud arguments that accompanied their drinking sessions almost invariably had to be settled by Grampa before he and the rest of the family could get any sleep.

The thought had crossed Grampa's mind more than once that maybe he ought to give Ervin Laird and Bo Pardue their walking papers. But the reality was, the third man he had working deserved the lion's share of the blame, and that man was Floyd Franklin. He was the one who set up the whiskey still in the wooded area to the rear of the house, completely ignoring Grampa's objections. Floyd was also the one who fueled the fires of dissension that flared up any time the men had idle time on their hands and whiskey in their bellies.

Considering that Floyd happened to be married to Edra, Grampa and Gramma's only daughter, Grampa could hardly afford to fire him. Floyd could not have supported the family without Grampa putting him to work.

Hearing the jangle of the harness coming closer, Grampa placed his hands against the tree and pulled himself to a standing position. He stretched to loosen his arthritis-stiffened joints before he made his way to the gate near the barn, meeting up with the men as they led their mules in from the field in the near total darkness.

"Y'all go on in the house and get supper," Grampa told his men. "I'll take the harness off these mules and feed 'n water 'em. You three have done enough for one day."

Exhausted, Ervin Laird stretched and exhaled loudly. "I do believe today is the hardest I ever worked in my life!"

Floyd was agreeing with Laird when something caught his eye. "Did y'all see that lightning way over yonder just now?"

"Yeah," agreed Bo and Ervin.

At nineteen, Bo was the youngest of the bunch, but that didn't seem to have given him any advantage; he was just as tired as either of the other men, including fifty-year-old Laird. With a crippled left arm, plowing was a real challenge and doubly tiring for Bo. He had broken his shoulder in a fall from the porch of his home when he was about five years old and the wound, left unattended, had rendered his arm virtually useless.

"I sure do appreciate y'all finishin' up," said Grampa, gathering all three lead ropes into one hand, and starting toward the gate leading to the barn.

Floyd, at twenty-eight, was in his prime, but it was very seldom that a man plowed for fourteen hours as hard and fast as those three had that day. He headed for the potato house near the main house where he had a bottle of his whiskey stashed. He was starving but supper was going to have to wait. Right now, he needed something to kill the pain.

Grampa approached the gate and stopped, watching Floyd as he walked away.

"Don't know how you forecasted the weather like that, Mr. Epps, but it looks like you hit the nail right on the head!" said Bo.

"I'll tell you something, son," Grampa said, turning back toward Bo, "When you've lived as long as I have, with nothin' to depend on but the Good Lord and this poor ground, you'll learn a few tricks yourself."

Laird laughed as he bent over to beat the dust from the legs of his overalls. "At the rate he's goin', Mr. Epps,

Bo won't near 'bout live to be as old as you are. He's just about dead already!"

"You may be right." Grampa laughed at Laird's remark as he led the mules on toward the barn.

The floor of the potato house was about three feet above the ground, and the crawlspace under the building was walled up completely, except for one rickety door that hung open, its corner sagging down, touching the ground. Floyd reached through the door, stretching his arm around and into the crawlspace. Groping around in the darkness for his bottle of whiskey, he placed his hand on something hairy and felt it move. He quickly jerked away his hand.

Growling and snarling, the dog bolted through the door, brushing against Floyd and frightening him so badly, he fell over backwards in his haste to avoid the dog.

"You dirty bastard!" Floyd muttered, as he picked himself up and watched the dog disappear into the darkness.

Laird was approaching and witnessed the commotion. Laughing, he said, "Floyd, you ain't scared of that dog, are you?"

"Hell, no!" Floyd retorted, angry to have Laird mocking him. "He just surprised me, that's all. It's time I load that mangy bastard in the wagon and haul him away from here. I don't know where he came from, but we don't need any more strays around here. And he's got the mange so bad, he's about dead anyway."

"A bullet would be a lot less trouble!"

"I don't want to kill him. I just want to be rid of him."

Floyd reached back into the crawlspace and found his bottle. He sat down on the ground, leaning back against the building so he could rest his aching back. He uncorked the bottle, but instead of taking a drink, he eased the bottle down beside his leg, and set it on the ground. "Boy, I'll tell you what," he said to Laird, "I'm glad this farmin's over for a while. This is my last bottle and I need to make some more in a hurry."

"Yeah, me too," said Laird, squatting down against the wall beside Floyd. "I'm going back to Sterlington in the morning and get the old lady so we can go on up the river and get them trotlines set out the first of the week."

"Epps thinks we're gonna make him rich," said Floyd, using Grampa's nickname, Epps. "He bought enough fishin' tackle for ten men. But just between you and me, fishin' on halves for him don't excite me too much. I can make twice as much money makin' whiskey, and have a hell of a lot more fun." (Fishing on halves meant that they got to keep half of the fish they caught, and whoever owned the boat and bought the hooks, lines, weight and bait, got to keep the other half. In this case, that was Grampa.)

"Well, I'm just gonna take it easy and do nothin' but run them trotlines," Laird ventured. "I don't care if I ever catch a damned fish!"

Laird kept his eye on the bottle, wondering if Floyd was ever going to get around to taking a drink. He reached over and punched him in the ribs, saying, "If you ain't gonna drink that damned stuff, hand it here! Hell, I'm thirsty!"

This irritated Floyd, but he didn't speak. He just looked straight ahead as he slowly raised the bottle and took a long drink, and then reluctantly passed the bottle to Laird. Floyd didn't like sharing with Laird at all. He had no idea how long he'd have to wait before he got the next bottle brewed, and he wanted this one to last as long as possible.

Laird had drifted in earlier that year, looking for work, and Grampa had hired him to help get the spring planting done. Floyd had taken an instant disliking to Laird, and the feeling was mutual. Floyd wasn't the kind of man who took much bullshit from any man, and Laird liked to throw his weight around.

From the very first day, Laird, with his overbearing personality, kept Floyd on edge. Floyd was much smaller in stature than Laird, and Laird liked to use this to his advantage. He got a kick out of quickly drawing back his arm like he was going to haul off and let him have it. Floyd instinctively dodged and ducked to avoid being struck, and each time he did, Laird got a satisfied smirk on his face.

This would incense Floyd. "Go ahead, you bastard! Try it! I'll take a goddamned club to you when you do!" He tried to use these inflated remarks to keep Laird from following up on his threats.

Now Laird was taking more than his fair share of Floyd's last bottle. Floyd reached up and jerked the bottle out of Laird's hand as he turned it up for what would have been his third long drink. "I'll tell you what, mister, if you want more whiskey, you'd better find a jug of your own!"

"Why, you wormy little son of a bitch!" Laird dragged the back of his hand across his chin to wipe away the whiskey, and got up from a squatting position. "I'll tear your ass up like a new-plowed field!"

Floyd was already on his feet, trying to place the cork in the bottle. "Come on, then!" he yelled, eyeing his surroundings for something he could use as a weapon. He was tired as hell but he had taken all he was going to take from this asshole.

Grampa had heard the argument begin and came running out of the barn, getting between the two adversaries. "Y'all just stop it right now! There ain't no sense in all this! Supper's waitin' so get on toward the house."

Grampa had used his sternest tone of voice, and it seemed to do the trick. Laird knew Grampa wasn't going to stand for any more nonsense, so he cleared his throat, turned his head aside to spit, and walked away toward the farmhouse without another word.

Bo stood in the doorway, looking back toward the barn until he saw the others coming, and then walked into the kitchen without speaking. Edra and Gramma sensed tension in the air. The two women already had beans and cornbread on the table, and Edra started pouring skim milk into glasses for the men to drink.

Bo had already taken a seat on the end of a bench alongside the long kitchen table, and the others filed in and sat down. Beginning with Grampa, they took turns spooning beans onto their plates. Then they ate in silence, save for the occasional grunting and pointing when someone wanted a dish passed their way. Once they had seen to it that the men had everything they needed, Edra and Gramma made their way to the front of the house.

When Laird finished his meal, he stood up and was about to head back out to the potato house where he and Bo used a clear corner for sleeping quarters, but Grampa raised his hand to get his attention. "Ervin, I need you to take me up to El Dorado, Arkansas on Monday if you can. I've got some business there."

"Yes, sir! I'll be glad to," he said, shooting a smug look at Floyd. He seemed to draw pleasure from the fact that he had a means of transportation and Floyd did not.

Floyd tried to ignore Laird as he finished eating and got up to leave the table. He got some satisfaction from knowing that Laird might have wheels, but he could have another shot of whiskey, all by himself, before retiring for the night. Meanwhile, Laird would be returning to Sterlington in the morning, to the Gregg farm on the

Ouachita River, and the little shanty he shared with his wife. Ever since hiring on, he had stayed on the Day farm during the week, and returned home to his wife each Sunday.

When Monday rolled around and Ervin Laird finally showed up to take Grampa to El Dorado, it was getting late in the morning. He had been drinking, and was loud and on the verge of being obnoxious as he swaggered toward the house. "Hell, I should've brought the old lady along!" he announced. "She likes to sit on her butt in the shade, too!"

This remark was directed at Edra and Gramma, who were sitting with their legs hanging off the edge of the porch, taking a break from their chores, and enjoying the shade from the nearby pecan tree. The two women didn't think Laird's remark was very funny, and they tried to ignore him, stretching their necks to see if Floyd was aware that Laird had arrived.

Floyd had seen Laird and heard his loud talking but from his position at the barn, it was hard to understand all that was being said. He decided to return to the house, knowing that he could probably expect a confrontation with Laird. As he started toward the house, Floyd saw the stray dog come sneaking out from under the porch, brushing against Edra's feet, surprising her, and causing her to kick her feet outwards. She gasped and clutched her heart with fake fright after she realized it was just the dog.

Remembering what Floyd had said on Saturday about wanting to be rid of the dog, Laird decided to do him a favor. He quickly reached out and grabbed the dog as he went skulking by him. The dog was a frail looking cur, so badly infected with the mange that half his fur had fallen out.

Laird had an evil grin on his face as he picked up the dog by the back legs and began viciously slamming him into the ground on his back. The dog was yelping as Laird beat the ground with him. The two women began screaming and shouting at Laird to stop his sickening display of cruelty.

"Hear! Hear!" Gramma shouted as she slid off the porch. "Don't you do that poor dog that way!" She stood there with her hands on her hips, horrified.

Laird ignored her completely, and continued beating the ground with the dog, fully intending to kill him before he stopped.

Grampa heard the commotion and appeared in the doorway. When he saw what was happening, he bounded down the steps, demanding that Laird stop his cruelty at once. Floyd had set off running toward Laird as soon as he saw Laird pick up the dog and begin beating him, and he and Grampa reached the cruel man at almost the same instant.

Floyd hit Laird across the side of his face, causing him to lose his hold on the dog and drop him to the ground, where he lay still, blood foaming from his nostrils.

As Laird tried to turn and get his hands on Floyd, he was caught by Grampa, who managed to hold him long enough to get between him and Floyd.

Grampa warned Floyd to get back, and continued to hold onto Laird's arms. "Now, you just hold on there, mister!" Despite being in his late fifties and suffering from arthritis and generally failing health, Grandpa had a good hold on Laird.

Floyd had stepped back a couple of feet, but despite the fact that Laird outweighed him by a good fifty pounds, he was still ready to fight. "I won't put up with this kind of stuff," he shouted. "Not in front of my wife!"

Grampa pointed Laird toward his panel truck parked near the dirt road that passed by the farm. "You go get in that truck and wait right there! Don't you make a move until I tell you. I mean it. Now, get on out there right now!"

Laird glared at Floyd for a few seconds and then obeyed Grampa's order, watching Floyd over his shoulder as he walked toward his truck.

Grampa walked over to his son-in-law. "Now, you just cool down, Floyd! That dog ain't worth having a killin' over and you know it!"

Floyd didn't respond. He only stood there, glaring at Laird.

Grampa turned toward his wife and daughter, calming them down and instructing them to go into the house. As they turned to go, he said, "Everything is alright now, so just go on. I have got to go to El Dorado, bad as I hate to ride with that drunk. But this business won't wait, so I'm goin'. It'll be nightfall before I get back, but don't y'all fret." He turned back toward Floyd for a few seconds, and then he began making his way toward Laird and the truck.

Floyd's eyes stayed fixed for a long moment on Laird, who was sitting behind the wheel of his panel truck. "What goes 'round comes 'round," he muttered to himself, as he turned to check on the dog. As he looked down at the poor mutt, and heard him gasping for what appeared to be his dying breath, Floyd cursed Laird.

He then started for the barn to hitch up the mules to the wagon, regretting that he had not done so the day before. He could have carried the dog up to Jim Ed Ward, who could doctor a dog and cure him from just about anything. Ward would have been glad to cure the mange on this one, using a mixture of sulfur, grease and God knows what else. It was a foul-smelling medicine that he mopped on with a rag tied to a stick. After two or three treatments, the mange would be cured and the dog's hair would grow back over the area that had been infected. Floyd didn't think the dog would live but he would try to get him to Jim Ed Ward in time anyway.

Then he turned his thoughts to the days ahead. There would come a time before too long when it would just be the two of them, him and Laird, out in the middle of nowhere. Maybe when they had their camps pitched at the river bottom for the summer of fishing. One way or another, there would come a time. Sooner or later, Laird would pay for what he had done.

Two

July, 1933

Ervin Laird had parked his truck and set up camp, a quarter mile downriver from Martin's Camp on the banks of the Ouachita River. Bo Pardue helped him erect a temporary shelter out of some scrap lumber. It was only a roof supported by four oak poles—something to provide shelter for Bo since Laird and his wife would be sleeping in their panel truck. It would also provide shade for them while cleaning any fish they might catch in the event that anyone came along wanting to buy some before they were hauled to market.

Floyd had pitched a tent a half mile away through the woods, near Mud Slough, along with his brother-in-law, Walter Smith. (Uncle Walter was married to Edra's half-sister, Ruth Day, whose mother was Grampa's first wife). Grampa had hired Uncle Walter, Floyd, Laird, and Bo to fish on halves after the cotton crop was plowed for the last time.

The slough looked like a bayou because it wound its way back through the woods a good ways, but the shallow water just stood there, the mud stirred up from the bottom by the alligator gar fish that thrashed about in search of food. This constant stirring created the light chocolate color of the water that gave the slough its name. The water backfed from the river provided its only source of water except for the rains that drained into it.

Almost a month had passed since the incident with the dog at the farm, and Floyd and Laird had argued about it a couple of times, nearly coming to blows on both occasions. Because they were both still working for Grampa, they had been together at times. Since they had been camped out in the swamp, their paths had not crossed often. When they did cross trails, Floyd would curse and threaten Laird, who wouldn't say much because both Floyd and Walter were always armed— Floyd with a double-barrel shotgun and Walter with a .22 rifle.

On the night of July 23rd, Floyd and Walter lay sleeping in the large homemade tent they had pitched beneath the tupelo gum trees alongside the slough. They slept peacefully, completely unaware that Laird and Bo were lurking nearby in the shadows cast by the dim moonlight through the trees. In his hand, Laird carried a huge hunting knife.

"If one of them moves," Laird whispered to Bo, "we're gonna have to kill them both. I'll get the first one and you hold the other one 'til I can help you. It's either them or us if they catch us! But we've got to get them guns, or the sons of bitches will shoot us, sooner or later!"

Bo had his face close to Laird in order to hear the whispered instructions. He nodded his head and strained his eyes toward the tent fifty feet ahead. He was reluctant to go through with it, but given the conditions that existed between the two camps, he felt it was probably necessary in order to avoid the violence that would surely result if there were a showdown.

Lately, in his conversations with Bo, Laird had been voicing threats against Floyd. On top of the confrontations the two had been having, Laird suspected Floyd of secretly meeting with his woman while he and Bo were on the river running their nets and trotlines. Laird was a big, burly man and his years had not diminished his strength. He was much stronger than his two intended victims. But knowing that Floyd and Walter always had their weapons, he had nixed any thoughts of starting a fight with them while they were awake.

"Let's move in a little bit closer," Laird said as he eased around the tree they had been standing behind. "We'll get to where we can hear 'em snorin'."

He placed his feet carefully and softly and motioned for Bo to follow. Then he moved his hand to his mouth to signal for quiet until they got within twenty feet of the tent and could hear the two men snoring, the sounds seemingly magnified by the darkness.

The nights were hot and humid, so the end of the tent was open except for a mosquito net. Without a net, no one could stay in the swamp at night unless they did as Bo did, submerging his body in the river's edge on a sandbar, with his head lying on the sand, just out from the water's edge. The mosquitoes didn't bother him much with just his face exposed, and having his body in the water while he slept gave him a cooler night's rest. It was a miracle the water moccasins didn't bother him; that was about the only danger he faced in sleeping this way.

Occasionally, he startled frog hunters drifting by boat along the river with their carbide lights strapped to their caps. The wavering flame of the carbide lanterns created eerie shadows anyway, and when a man's head and nothing else suddenly appeared out of the shadows, it could be rather alarming.

During the cold days of winter when Bo was alone on the river, he would drag two logs to within a few feet of one another and set them afire. When nightfall came, he would throw sand on them to extinguish most of the flames, leaving the logs glowing like charcoal. He would then lie down between the logs for a warm, comfortable night's sleep in the sand. During this time when the Depression was public enemy number one, a man survived any way he could.

"Let's go," whispered Laird, once he was sure that both Floyd and Walter were sleeping soundly.

He and Bo immediately lowered themselves to the ground and crawled the remaining distance, inching along silently to the front corner of the tent. This was no easy feat for either man. Laird's bulk and the huge knife in his right hand hindered him while crawling. He had made the knife himself, supposedly to match his size, but it was too large even for him. He liked to boast that he could cut off a man's head with only one swipe of the knife. He honed the knife almost daily, and it usually took only a few strokes on his razor strap to bring back the razor-sharp edge. Floyd and Walter knew that Laird had never cut anyone with his knife, but they still had great respect for this weapon.

Bo's crippled left arm impeded his progress. But the years of farm laboring had given him amazing strength in his good arm, and there was no doubt in his mind about his ability to handle Walter or Floyd if trouble arose that night.

Laird carefully and silently untied the side of the mosquito net and pushed it aside. As planned, he moved inside to the side of the tent where Floyd lay. Bo followed and crawled toward Walter. In the dim light, Laird could barely see. When his eyes did become adjusted to the darkness inside the tent, he saw Floyd sleeping on his side with his back toward the middle of the tent. His shotgun lay beside him, the barrel pointing toward the front of the tent.

Laird reached for the gun with his left hand and, as his fingers encircled the barrel, Floyd made a gasping sound and his snoring abruptly stopped. Laird tensed up, his grip frozen around the barrel of the gun. Floyd began to stir, slowly rolling over onto his back. As he did, Laird quickly raised his right hand high, aiming the tip of his knife in the general direction of Floyd's heart. Walter's snoring was the only sound for several seconds while Laird held his position and Bo watched in fear of what might happen next.

Then, as suddenly as it had stopped, Floyd's snoring began again. But Laird still had a problem, for Floyd's left leg lay across the gun barrel and Laird's left hand. He held his breath as he relaxed his grip on the gun barrel and slowly pulled his hand out from underneath Floyd's leg. He felt a great sense of relief when he had succeeded in doing this without waking Floyd—but now, there was no way to get the gun. He eased back slowly and sat against his heels, looking over at Bo with a blank expression on his face.

Bo was having better luck on the other side of the tent. Walter's rifle lay a couple of feet to one side, and Bo gingerly picked it up and held it close, turning to watch Laird for any signal he might make. He was relieved to see the signal to leave.

Their departure was as slow and silent as their arrival had been, and once they were clear of the camp, they stopped to discuss the possibility of returning to the tent and taking the other gun by force.

"We ain't done a damned bit of good," Laird commented as he eased himself down to sit on a log. "We need to get Floyd's shotgun! He's the one I don't trust."

"I guess you're right," said Bo, as he placed the rifle butt on the ground and leaned the barrel against a tree. "We ought to go back, slip in there, and knock them out. They won't ever know who did it and they won't be brave enough without their guns to accuse us of doin' it."

"Goddamn, Bo," said Laird, "if you ain't about a dumb son of a bitch! These damned woods ain't just overrun with people, you know?" He turned his head to one side and spit. "What we gotta do is catch them off guard again and get the shotgun then. I don't want to have to kill 'em , but I'll tell you one thing, if I catch Floyd messin' round my woman, I'll kill him on the spot for sure! I done seen how he flirts with her every chance he gets." Laird grunted softly as he stood up, then he stretched and started down the trail toward his camp. "Hell, let's get back to camp and go to bed."

Bo was not quite ready to hit the river for his nightly soaking while Laird piled into the back of his panel truck with his woman. "Hey," he said. "I'll tell you what we can do! I found out where Floyd and Walter been makin' whiskey over there across the river! It's up yonder around the first bend in the river, about a hundred yards out in the woods. You know where them old vines are so thick? Right around there. If we go get what whiskey they got made, we can get drunk tonight. Then we can sell the rest of it when we go to town."

Floyd and Walter had been making the whiskey to sell, and of course, they'd been drinking some of it, as well. That afternoon when Bo found the still, he had sipped some of the sour mixture he called beer from the barrel of mash, and now he was craving some of the whiskey. He had been too scared to disturb the whiskey at the time, but now his thirst was overruling his better judgment.

"Now, why in the hell didn't you tell me that before dark?" Laird said.

Bo could see the disgusted look on his partner's face in the moonlight as he turned around to scold him.

"...We could be stumblin' drunk or passed out by now instead of just wanderin' around out here in the damned woods!" After making Bo think he was really mad, Laird laughed and gave Bo a friendly slap across his back. "Come on, let's go get drunk!"

They began to walk back to their camp through the woods. Then Bo broke away from the trail to find a hollow log where he could hide the rifle. He planned to return for it when he made a trip to town, so that he could take it to his father's home. He had always wanted a rifle of his own—a gun he could actually shoot. His father had only a shotgun, and Bo had trouble shooting a shotgun with his handicap.

When they came to the camp, Laird went to the panel truck and got his shotgun out without disturbing his woman who lay asleep in the truck. He then strode toward the river, catching up to Bo, who was already approaching the boat he had pulled up onto the sandbar after running his fishing lines that morning.

It would be an hour before they would get to quench their thirst. First they had to drag the heavy wooden boat into the river and paddle upstream for thirty minutes. Then, they had to guide the boat over to the riverbank. Bo looped the tie rope over a limb on the pecan tree which had fallen into the water when the river's current had undercut its base, and finally they were free to go after the liquor.

They stumbled through the woods, fighting the vines and mosquitoes for over half an hour as they searched for the still. They were on the verge of giving up the search when Bo finally found what he was looking for. They immediately helped themselves to the whiskey—making them the first ones to sample the first batch made by Floyd and Walter since they'd camped out on the river to fish.

The two men didn't linger long at the still. The mosquitoes were especially vicious while the men were not moving around. This prompted Laird to give the order to gather up the jugs of whiskey and move out toward the boat.

"These damned mosquitoes must not have had anything to eat for a month!" Laird said, fighting them off with one hand while reaching for a jug with the other.

Bo was in full agreement as he gathered up two jugs with his good arm and hooked a finger of the hand on his crippled arm through the loop of another.

With great difficulty, they made their way through the vine strewn thicket to the riverbank and their boat. Laird held the boat steady while Bo gingerly stepped inside. He moved toward the rear, wobbling and weaving as he stepped over the paddles and fishing gear.

Laird took the rope from the limb it was tied to, placed one knee on the bow of the boat, and shoved away from the bank with his other foot, crawling and falling gracelessly into the boat as it shot away from the river's edge. Once he got settled in the front seat, he handed his shotgun to Bo and reached for a jug. He and Bo each uncorked their jugs and began drinking more whiskey as they drifted downstream.

Having quenched their thirst temporarily, they picked up the hand-hewn oak paddles and turned the boat toward the middle of the river where they could get the full effect of the moon's light, away from the shadows along the riverbanks.

Only a few minutes had passed when Laird stopped paddling, took another drink, and then started to laugh. "I'll make a bet that Floyd and Walter will be mad as hell when they find their whiskey missin'!"

He reached into his shirt pocket for his sack of tobacco, slipped the packet of papers from under the band of the tobacco sack, and slid a paper off the stack. After pouring the tobacco, he pulled the drawstring tight with his teeth and put the sack back into his pocket. He began slowly rolling the cigarette and then turned his head to the side where Bo could hear him more clearly. "I'm about out of tobacco. I'd better go up to Martin's in the morning and get some."

Bo listened, but said nothing. He was thinking about everything he'd gotten himself mixed up in that night, and he was feeling more than a little uneasy about it. The light from Laird's match as he lit his cigarette interrupted Bo's thoughts and brought him back to the present.

"Yeah," said Bo, "I'll bet they will be raisin' hell, especially after they find that rifle missin'. We may have to whup 'em 'cause you know they're gonna blame it all on us."

He then took another drink and after swallowing the moonshine, he began shaking his head from side to side. "Whew! That stuff sho' is stout! And it don't go down no easier after you been drinkin' it a while!"

Laird chuckled at Bo. "Well, I'll tell you something," he said, his mood suddenly turning serious, "if Floyd says one damned thing to me about it, I'm gonna blow his head right off his shoulders! That's why I got my shotgun loaded with buckshot!" The whiskey was having an effect on Laird's thinking, and Bo had been around him long enough to know how nasty he could be when he was drinking.

Bo had also known and worked with Floyd and Walter ever since the two men had moved to nearby Dean Community. He didn't want any trouble with them. In addition to generating some extra cash, this fishing trip was supposed to separate the men from each other, lessening the chance of trouble between them. That's why Grampa had arranged it so Floyd and Walter were camping at one place, and Bo and Laird were camping at another.

The trip was also supposed to give the family some relief from the drinking and bickering that seemed inevitable whenever Bo, Laird, and Floyd were together. Now Bo realized that he may be causing more trouble than he had bargained for. Since Floyd and Laird had become such bitter enemies, Bo now sensed real danger in the situation that was developing. And he felt that he was to blame for it because he had stolen the gun and whiskey.

The moon was being obliterated by fast moving clouds, and the moonlight was being replaced by the glow of lightning across the sky. A chilling rain was soon falling and Laird cursed as he began paddling furiously downstream, correcting his course when the lightning allowed him a view of the river ahead.

The two men were silent during the remainder of the dreary trip downriver, lost in their thoughts. As they made their way to the camp, Bo realized he'd better sleep for the rest of the night on the fish-cleaning table under the shed they had erected. That would protect him from the rain—but they still needed protection from the confrontation that would surely come with the morning light.

Not wanting to be a party to a killing, Bo picked up Laird's shotgun and eased it over the side of the boat, placing it beneath the water's surface to prevent a telltale splash, and softly let it slip from his grip. He might have gotten rid of Laird's rifle too, but it wasn't in the boat with them.

He felt much better after doing this, secure in the knowledge that his actions might very well prevent a killing. He also felt he could convince Laird that the shotgun had been accidentally knocked overboard when he discovered it missing. He took another drink of whiskey to warm him from the rain's chilling effects.

Three

July, 1933

The rain continued falling during the night, and morning brought more of the same. This awakened Walter earlier than usual. As soon as he opened his eyes, he discovered his rifle missing. He seldom let his rifle out of his sight, so he realized at once that someone must have stolen it during the night. He began cursing as he awakened Floyd and told him of his discovery.

Floyd sat bolt upright. "Laird and Bo! Them dirty bastards! They have really got a lot of damned nerve, comin' in on us while we're asleep. It's a wonder they didn't kill us! If I hadn't been sleepin' on my shotgun, they would have stolen it too!" Floyd was even more upset than Walter, perhaps because he had more to fear from Laird, who had been threatening him.

Their first inclination was to barrel into the other camp and demand the return of the rifle. But after discussing it further, they decided to wait until the rain subsided. That way, they could check on their mash and have a good drink of whiskey before the showdown.

Floyd looked toward the slough and then toward the trail leading through the woods in the direction of the river north of their camp. "Let's walk through and borrow Gordon Martin's boat. That will save us a bunch of damned paddlin'."

"Now, why didn't I think of that?" Walter looked almost as if he were apologizing for not doing so. "Let's go."

A light rain was still falling when Floyd raised his shotgun, rested it across his shoulder, and started down the trail to the river. Walter fell in silently behind him.

They had to pass by Laird's camp on their way to the river. As they approached, Laird called out to Walter. "Hey, if y'all are goin' up to Martin's, how about pickin' me up a sack of tobacco?"

Walter did an excellent job of hiding his anger as he walked over to Laird and accepted the quarter he offered. "I'll get you some, but it might be an hour or two before we get back."

"Okay," said Laird, as he watched Walter catch up with Floyd and make their way along the slippery trail that disappeared around the bend of the river. He guessed that they were going to their still and figured they would be in a lot less agreeable mood when they returned. He was relieved that they had not mentioned the missing gun.

Floyd took the lead as they made their way along the narrow trail by the river where the bank dropped sharply, like a cliff, to the river twenty feet below. He carefully scanned the wet trail for any sign of movement, ever mindful of the many snakes along the river. They followed the winding path to Gordon Martin's camp—a weather-beaten shack mounted on huge logs and strapped together to float it closer to high ground when the backwaters flooded the swamp.

The river was below its pool stage now, so the shack was sitting atop a gently sloping bank at the point where Frank La Pierre Creek ran into the river. Despite the colorful name of the creek, the campsite was known simply as The Mouth of the Creek to everyone in the area.

Gordon Martin's camp served as a store for the people on the river. He kept tobacco, canned goods, crackers, and other items on hand, both as a supply for himself and as a means of bolstering his income when fishing was not good.

As he and Floyd arrived at the camp, Walter stepped up on the log step placed against the front porch of the shack. With a grunt, he made the high step onto the porch, greeting Gordon as he approached the door. Floyd walked over to the water's edge and gazed out across the river.

"After all this rain," Gordon said, pointing toward the river, "fishin' ain't gonna be worth a flip for two or three days. I don't think I'll even run my nets today." The flow of muddy water from the creek was making jagged lines as it changed the river's color from murky green to a khaki color in a streak that grew wider as it flowed downstream, gradually changing to green again as it blended in with the flow of the river.

Gordon turned and stepped inside his shack, followed by Walter.

"Yeah, that rain did mess us up. I think I'll just finish that net I been weavin'," said Walter, while searching in his pocket for the quarter Laird had given him. "Give me a sack of tobacco." He handed Gordon the quarter and stuffed the change and tobacco into the bib of his overalls.

"Gordon, me and Floyd figured we might be able to borrow your boat for a little while to go across the river," said Walter, stepping down from the porch and looking back over his shoulder at the storekeeper.

"Yeah, go right ahead, 'cause I sure ain't goin' out today. I'm strictly gonna mind the store." Gordon smiled faintly—a change from his usual glum expression. He was a man who simply did not smile often.

"We appreciate it," said Floyd, as he and Walter stepped into Gordon's wide-bottom boat. "It sure beats paddlin' out Mud Slough in our boat, and all the way up here against that current!"

Mud Slough ran into the river downstream of Gordon's store. So they would have had to paddle down the slough to the river, and then upstream for a few hundred yards to get to that point. Then they would have had to continue paddling upstream to the point where their whiskey still was, had they used their own boat to make the trip.

Floyd picked up a wooden scoop from the floor of the boat and began dipping out the rain water covering the floor.

"We won't be gone long," Walter yelled to Gordon as he and Floyd shoved the boat away from the shore. They began paddling by the neck of the opposite creek bank and into the river, staying close to the river bank and out of the main current for a hundred yards or so upstream before crossing over. Some of their anger had subsided upon anticipation of a soothing drink of their own creation.

They made their way through the wet bushes and vines. As they got closer and closer to the still, they could almost taste their whiskey. At last they were at the still— but instead of finding their supply, they discovered their whiskey missing. They became enraged, and began cursing Laird and Bo all over again, Floyd vowing to beat both of them half to death.

They removed the ragged canvas covering from the barrel of mash. Then Floyd took the tin cup which hung from the rim of the barrel on an S-hook fashioned from a piece of baling wire, and dipped it into the mash, letting only the liquid flow over the cup's edge until it was nearly full. He stopped his grumbling long enough to take a drink of the sour liquid. It packed a wallop but it was rough tasting and when consumed in quantity, the aftereffects—mainly an extremely upset stomach—could last for days.

Passing the cup back and forth, Floyd and Walter continued to vent their anger. After several refills, they began to feel the effects of the alcohol. They placed the canvas cover over the barrel, camouflaging it with brush so it would stay hidden, and headed back to the boat for the trip back to Gordon Martin's, and then on to Laird's camp. As they made their way along, vengeance weighed heavily on their minds.

When they returned to Gordon's camp, they told him of their suspicions concerning Laird and Bo, but said nothing of their intentions. They quickly thanked Gordon for the use of his boat and headed out along the trail toward Laird's camp. They were ready for a showdown.

Traversing the trail along the river, they met a rider who, seeing them approach, stopped his horse and dismounted. Coming closer, they recognized Roy Nash and greeted him. The passage of time had intensified the effects of the mash they had consumed, and now Floyd began voicing threats against Laird and Bo, telling Roy about the loss during the night of the gun. Floyd didn't mention the missing whiskey, figuring it was safer to keep it to himself. There was a good chance Roy already knew about the private still, but if he didn't, Floyd wanted to leave it that way.

Roy sympathized with them but commented little about their misfortune before mounting his horse to ride away and leave the two men to resume their journey.

When Floyd and Walter entered Laird's camp, they had one thing on their minds—demanding the return of their goods. Getting straight to the point, Walter walked up to Bo, who was sitting on the tailgate of the truck with Laird, and demanded the return of his rifle.

Bo denied any knowledge of the missing rifle or the accusations being directed at him.

"Boy, I'll wipe this ground with you if you don't come up with that rifle!" Walter said through clenched teeth. With a menacing, unblinking stare, he moved closer to Bo, stopping within six inches of his face. Walter was only five-feet-six-inches tall, considerably shorter than Bo. But he was similar to Floyd in stature—tough and wiry—and there would be no backing down on his part. He intended to either reclaim his rifle or whip Bo, or maybe both.

"Hold it!" said Laird, reaching over and grabbing Bo's arm. "Bo, if you got his damned rifle, give it back to him."

Bo swung around, staring for a moment at Laird with a confused look on his face. He was shocked at this command, but he stood up and slowly walked away toward the trail leading to the other camp. Nobody spoke as he disappeared into the woods, reappearing within five minutes with Walter's rifle, which he handed over without a word.

Laird thought his show of righteousness would fool Floyd and Walter and maybe keep them from blaming the missing whiskey on him and Bo, but he was mistaken. Floyd had been building up his nerve while waiting for Bo to return with the gun. Seeing Bo hand over the rifle was the catalyst he needed to proceed with his initial plans.

"Now that we got that out of the way," he said, "I got a few things to say. We knew y'all stole Walter's gun and we know too that y'all stole all our whiskey from up at our still. And, I'm mad as hell! I want it all back and I want it right now!"

"Now you just hold on there for a minute!" Laird held up his right hand to stop Floyd from speaking. "I didn't know Bo had stolen that rifle and I damned sure don't know nothin' about no whiskey! And by the way, while you're talkin' about this kind of shit, I see you got some of my boards down at your camp and you done cut 'em up. Now, I want my boards, and when you bring 'em back, they better be back together!"

For a moment, Floyd stared at him in disbelief. "I'll bring your boards back, but you know damned well I can't put 'em back together! But right now I want my goddamned whiskey, you lyin' son of a bitch!"

"You look here now!" Laird pointed a threatening finger at Floyd, unfazed by the double-barrel shotgun cradled in Floyd's arms. "Don't you call me a lyin' son of a bitch! I'll cut your damned heart out!" Laird matched Floyd's nasty tone.

"Y'all settle down now," Bo said, scared. He saw Laird eyeing his rifle which lay in the far side of the truck, along with his big knife. Bo had taken the shells out of the rifle earlier when Laird had gone into the woods to relieve himself. He put his hand into his pocket and fingered the shells nervously, hoping Laird wasn't planning to go for his gun.

Neither man seemed to hear Bo, so he retreated to a huge oak tree about thirty feet away and leaned against it, hoping the argument would die down. He realized that Laird had not yet discovered that his rifle had no shells in it. The actions Bo had taken that morning and the night before to disarm Laird were done to discourage him from challenging Floyd. But now Bo realized that trouble was developing too quickly for his plan to work. At that point, he was afraid to say or do a thing.

Suddenly, Laird shifted toward the gun and the knife, grasping for a weapon while keeping his eyes on Floyd. The big knife was closer to him than the gun, and as his hand closed around the bone handle, Floyd cocked both hammers on his shotgun.

Laird's woman had walked over to the back of the truck and was standing near him. She started to speak but was interrupted by Floyd as he leveled his shotgun toward Laird and shouted, "Stand back, Grandma!" (Floyd and Walter had jokingly hung the nickname of Grandma on her when she first came to Dean with her common-law husband, Laird.)

When the woman turned to get out of the way, she saw Walter running toward the cover of the trees at the edge of the clearing. This prompted her to run toward the river, not really knowing where she was running to, or why.

Bo had eased around behind the tree he had been leaning against, but when he saw the others running, he turned to run, himself. He was only a few feet from his original position when the shot rang out.

Laird was making his way out of the truck bed, and his feet had barely touched the ground when the shotgun went off. The blast caught him in the left side of his face, blowing his jaw away and rocking him back against his camping gear piled in the rear of the truck. His legs dangled limply from the tailgate of the truck and the knife fell from his hand, falling in almost the exact position where it had lain a moment earlier.

The others had stopped running and turned toward the camp as the sound of gunfire echoed through the trees. They saw Floyd, not moving, with the gun still pointed at Laird. A few seconds passed, dragging as if they were minutes. Still afraid to come too close, the three deserters were cautiously inching their way back toward the camp, relying on the cover of trees around the clearing.

There was a moan from the truck, barely audible, as Laird slowly brought his left hand up to his face and pressed his open palm against the ugly wound, holding it there until the blood ran between his fingers and down the back of his hand. He moaned again, this time a little bit stronger, and made a failed attempt to sit up.

Floyd knew that the first shot would have caused a slow, torturous death for Laird, and he had to end his victim's suffering. In a panic, he ran around to the side of the truck and pointed the gun through the open back window of the truck. He fired another blast into the top of the wounded man's head, shooting from behind because he could not bear to face the horrifying sight he had created with his first shot. Strangely enough, Floyd's second shot, with its instant death, brought mercy for Laird.

The roar of the shotgun echoed across the swamp, signaling to all within range, humans and animals alike. It was a call to silence, an eerie moment of quiet and stillness that brought to Floyd the realization that he had just created the ultimate tragedy—the taking of another man's life. In the next few moments, the full effect of what he had done settled itself down in the front row of his memory, always to be there, an eternal reminder that, of all the mistakes he had ever made, there was but one that could never be rectified.

The scene would reenact itself in his mind periodically from that point forward, appearing many times when least expected, and leaving him yearning for relief from the tragic memory—relief that was nowhere to be found.

JUDGMENT

STATE OF LOUISIANA
vs.
Floyd Franklin
....
....

NO. _7156_,

PARISH OF JACKSON,

STATE OF LOUISIANA,

THIRD JUDICIAL DISTRICT COURT.

THE ACCUSED.

Floyd Franklin .... age _28_ years,
.... age .... years,
.... age .... years,

having been regularly convicted of the crime of:

N. V. Manslaughter
....
....
.... 'r' ....
....;

IT IS THEREFORE ORDERED that the said accused be imprisoned in the Louisiana State Penitentiary, at hard labor, for a period of not less than _two_ years nor more than _six_ years, (each,) and that (he) (they and each of them) pay a fine of ....
.... DOLLARS—and all cost of this prosecution.

This judgment is subject to commutation for good time service according to law.

— DONE, READ AND SIGNED in open Court, on this the _19_ _th_ .... day of
February .... , 193_4_ .

.... _E. L. Flaser_ ....
Judge, Third Judicial District Court of Louisiana.

STATE OF LOUISIANA   In Third Judicial District Court,

vs.   Parish of Union,

Floyd Franklin   State of Louisiana.

STATEMENT OF TRIAL JUDGE.

Charge:- This defendant was charged with the crime of murder,
          was tried and convicted of manslaughter, with recommendation
          of mercy by the jury.

Character:-   So far as I am able to learn, and I think my informa-
          tion is correct, the defendant has not been convicted of any
          offense against the law prior to this time. Other than his
          connection with illicit liquor transactions, which, to some
          extent, entered into the cause of the commission of this
          crime, he appears to have been, theretofore, a rather harm-
          less farmer. I do not think he will give the authorities
          of the penitentiary any trouble.
          Ruston, La., March 5, 1934.

                         Respectfully submitted,

                         _E. _____ JUDGE._

                         J U D G E.

Four

1976

D ecades after the killing, I would be working as a salesman for a piping supply firm and on a hot July afternoon, I would decide to take some cold beer to a pipeline crew laying some of the pipe I had sold. The pipeline ran through the swamp which paralleled the Ouachita River only a couple miles from where I was born. The superintendent over the job suggested that I stop on my way out of the swamp and offer some of the leftover beer to Bo Pardue.

I had heard of Bo in years past but had never met him, so I was pretty interested in doing so. I vaguely recalled hearing Gramma talk about the time when Bo worked for Grampa and Boo McCormick, our neighbor. Like a lot of people, I had a fondness for the past and for old-timers in particular, so spending the afternoon with an old-timer from my family's past seemed like a good way to spend the rest of the afternoon. I could never have guessed what ramifications this chance meeting would have for me.

I pulled over and stopped the car when I came to the old dilapidated houseboat which had obviously been dry-docked on a ridge—the highest ground in the immediate area—during a period of high water. The river was about two hundred yards to the north of the ridge.

As I walked toward the houseboat through the woods which were littered with cans and other debris, Bo came out to investigate. A dark brown cur dog with his hackles slightly raised sized me up with a wary eye as I shook hands with Bo, introduced myself and offered him a beer.

Bo sized me up and with a reserved tone said, "Yeah, I guess I'll have one. You one of Floyd's boys?"

"Yeah, I'm the seventh son comin' down the line," I replied as I walked toward the car, looking back over my shoulder at Bo. "I've been down to the end of the pipeline with a few refreshments for the crew and I had some left over. Jimmy Rogers thought you might want some, hot as this weather is."

Bo appeared to be in his mid-sixties, and was tough looking with several days' growth of whiskers. His left arm hung limp at his side. "Boy, they are really goin' to town with that pipeline, ain't they? That Rogers feller, he's a go-getter."

I handed him a beer from the ice chest in the back of the car and started to lift the tab on my own. "Yeah, they're movin' on."

Bo looked up the pipeline right-of-way toward the river with a faraway look in his eyes and immediately began recalling the past. "Yeah, I knowed Floyd well. I used to live down there with Mr. Epps Day, your grand-daddy, when I was not much more than a kid. I helped him farm and me and Floyd used to make whiskey together. I never did see Floyd after he went to prison for killin' that feller, though." He paused to take a sip of his beer and was silent for a moment, gazing toward the river.

The mention of the killing sparked my interest immediately. All I knew about it at that point in time was that my father had killed a man and had spent some time in the state prison at Angola in the southern part of Louisiana. I had never learned more about the killing than that, because no one wanted to tell me when I was a child and as I grew older, I didn't pursue it. It was only after my parents had passed away that I felt a need to know more about the past.

"Do you know what happened—why he killed that fellow?" As I asked him the question, I doubted that Bo had any idea just how badly I wanted to know the answer.

Walking over to a huge oak tree, Bo sat down on a root that sloped away from the base of the tree for three feet before entering the ground. "Yeah, I saw it when it happened. I was camped out right up yonder, the other side of Mud Slough, with the man he killed. Me and him had a camp three or four hundred yards from your daddy's and your uncle Walter's camp. Well, that fellow had a camp—I just sort'a stayed around with him most of the time."

Bo had stated it matter-of-factly, but his statement made an astounding impact on me. There I was, trying to put together a story from almost nothing, and I had by mere chance stumbled upon someone who could tell me all about it—if only he would! I was very excited over the possibility of learning from Bo some facts I'd been longing to know for years. Not wanting to give Bo the impression I was overly interested in the subject, I tried to appear calm, and asked, "Would you mind telling me all about it?"

Taking another sip of his beer, Bo set the can on the ground beside me and wiped his lips with the back of his good hand. He looked away for a few seconds and then looked back at me, shaking his head from side to side. "Naw, I don't mind, if you think you want to hear it."

"Hell, yeah, I would like to hear it!" I replied. "I've always wondered just what took place and for some reason, nobody ever told me."

Taking an occasional sip of his beer, Bo shared his recollections of what took place the morning of the killing and during the weeks preceding it. I listened intently to Bo's story and as he told of disposing of the shotgun in the river that night, and emptying the rifle of its shells, I realized that I quite possibly owed my own existence to this tough old guy who now lived alone in the swampland, almost like a hermit. It gave me kind of a haunting feeling to know that, in essence, Ervin Laird's life may have been sacrificed for my own in the same section of swampland where I stood that afternoon. It was an extremely sobering realization as I began to understand the significance of it all.

Bo looked at me in silence for a few seconds and made what appeared to be his final statement concerning those events of so long ago. "I believe that Floyd was scared of that man."

I sensed that Bo had told me all he wanted to about the incident, so I changed the subject. "Bo, what happened to your arm?" I was thinking I should not have asked, but my curiosity usually overruled my better judgment.

"I fell off the front porch when I was about five year old and broke my shoulder," he replied as he moved his right hand up to his drooping left shoulder and began to rub his arm from the shoulder down to the elbow. "I broke this shoulder right in the joint and it didn't heal right. They didn't have much in the way of doctors then, you know. I never did have much use of it after that, but I guess I did alright."

We had both finished our beers by this time, so I made a quick trip to the car for more. During this short break in the conversation, I thought about what Bo had told me and wondered again what might have happened if Bo had not disposed of that shotgun that night and emptied the rifle of its shells—a question that could never be answered.

I knew that Bo had only recently returned to the area to live, and I was curious about where he had spent his adult life up to that point. As I returned with the beer, I asked, "Where did you go when you left this part of the country, Bo?"

He slowly turned the can of beer in his hand until the tab was pointing away from him and then placed it between his knees to hold it while he lifted the tab. It opened with a "whoosh" and he took a long swallow.

"Well, I just sort'a bummed around for a while. I hoboed out to California and met a feller named Texas Pete when I was hitching a ride in a boxcar. He was sort'a King of the Hobos. I seen a railroad dick hit him with an ax handle. That bastard took a cut at me and I dodged him, and then he come at Pete. He busted his head wide open and throwed him off the train while it was rollin' there across New Mexico." Bo rambled on with his arm waving and his eyes gleaming as he stared off into the distance, as if it were all flashing before him on a movie screen.

"That dick thought I jumped out the door, I reckon, 'cause I had run thataway when he cut at me with that ax handle. But I sidestepped about the time he swung at Pete and dived over behind a bunch of feed stacked up in sacks, you know? I was lucky he didn't get after me again 'cause he was a big man and he would'a probably killed me, too! He must'a thought I was a damned idiot, if he was a thinkin' I jumped off that train doin' forty miles an hour!"

Bo stopped talking long enough to lift the beer and take a drink. Then he toned his voice down and began again. "California didn't show me too much so I headed back east. I lived up at Camden, Arkansas and fished for a livin' for a year or two on the river there. Then I wound up in Little Rock. I went to work for a rich feller there a takin' care of his yard and landscapin'. I knowed a lot about growin' stuff, you know, what with all my farmin' experience. And I was purty good at it, too! I stayed on there and helped that man with his business, too, 'til I finally decided to retire and come home. I guess now I'll be right here 'til I'm gone."

I sipped my beer and listened for nearly another hour as Bo recounted experiences from his boyhood right up to an altercation he had been involved in recently with a colorful old character very much like himself, who lived in a shack on the riverbank nearby. Bo had become an enemy simply by being brazen enough to move within two hundred yards of him and then use the man's personal launching area to dock his fishing boat. The other man didn't seem to place much stock in the fact that both the land and the launching area were public areas.

The man's nastiness about Bo's so-called intrusion on "his" place led to a fight between them. One day, two brothers—young men who were part time fishermen, part time roughnecks in the oil field, and full time hell raisers—took Bo's side in the argument and wound up pistol-whipping the old man, putting him in the hospital.

"He ain't bothered me none since," said Bo, gazing out toward the river.

I hoped Bo would voice disapproval of the young men's tactics against such an old man, even if he was still pretty tough for his age. But Bo said nothing about his defenders. He remained silent for a couple of minutes, and his silence gave me the impression that he wanted to say something but simply couldn't bring himself to bad-mouth people who had befriended him in their own twisted way.

When it came time for me to go, I would have found it difficult had it not been for those dreaded mosquitoes that had begun their daily assault on all living creatures, the encroaching darkness causing their numbers to multiply. I thanked Bo for the visit and left him swatting mosquitoes from his face with his good arm.

As I drove away down the dusty pipeline right-of-way, I began to think more about what Bo had told me about my father, and it brought to mind my earliest memories of him as well as the happy times and sad times I experienced during that period in my life when I began to become fully aware of where our relationship as father and son was headed.

Not knowing a lot about Floyd or his past, I thought about what little history I did have on him. One of the few pieces of my father's backstory I was privy to related to his middle name, Kinsolving. Apparently, Floyd's mother admired a notable doctor by the same name that lived in the St. Louis, Missouri area where Floyd was reared.

As a child, Floyd had been brought up in a series of lumber camps, where his mother was a cook. She reportedly weighed three hundred pounds and had a reputation for being just as mean as she wanted to be. I never knew my paternal grandmother and considering the talk I heard about her, maybe it was better that way.

The single piece of information I possessed about Floyd's father was that his name was Sir John Franklin and he was born in Elmira, New York in 1864.

I knew that Floyd had appeared here in Union Parish during the 1920s as a hobo who left the train at the small community of Dean to visit my uncle, Walter, who was a cousin of his. I was to find out in later years that Floyd was actually AWOL from the United States Marines and never returned to the base in New Jersey where he had been stationed when he received the weekend pass that turned into a lifetime pass for him. (He turned himself in when World War II was declared, and received something less than an honorable discharge.)

While at Dean he met Edra Day, who was a half sister to Walter's wife. They were married soon afterwards and lived with her parents, John Edward (Grampa) and Sarah Elizabeth (Gramma). At the time of the killing, there had been four children born to Floyd and Edra, with only three surviving, and when Floyd went to prison, the burden of caring for his family was placed on Grampa, whose health was not very good.

After a couple of years of fighting the hardships, the situation was beginning to look hopeless for Grampa and Gramma. They could not sufficiently feed or clothe the children, who were on the verge of suffering from malnutrition. Even though Grampa had suffered much abuse and humiliation from Floyd in the past, he went to the trial judge and pleaded with him for help, promising to do everything within his power to keep Floyd in line if only he could get him out of prison somehow. The judge managed to set the machinery in motion for a pardon, which came a few months later.

I was driving slowly away from Bo's and down the road leading toward home when I drove by the old homestead. Looking at it, I saw a place that was much different than it was then, as was almost everything. In my mind, I pictured the old house. It was made of logs and had a chimney of bricks, clay and straw, and by the time I had arrived on the scene, the wooden shingles that had originally covered it were replaced by a tin roof. It was there in that old house that eleven Franklin children were born. Only Ricky, the youngest, had the privilege of being born in a clinic.

(My mother actually gave birth to *ten* boys and two girls, but the firstborn was a son named Randolph Franklin who died at birth. He is buried in a small cemetery in a field a couple of miles from where we lived. Floyd made an aluminum marker and attached it to a wooden stake and over the years, the stake rotted, leaves and brush covered the cemetery, and now the marker is lost. In recent years someone has cut the brush and trees and begun to keep the grass mowed. I'm sure the marker was covered with several inches of rotted leaves when the cleanup was done, and the grass grew over everything afterwards. I think there are about seventeen gravesites with some type of stone markers there. I intend to buy a metal detector and go to the area soon, and try to find the marker. I saw the marker that Floyd put on the grave when I was a teenager, so I know the area that I need to search. I hope I can find its location so I can place a proper marker there.)

The old house was built after the turn of the century, and I remember Gramma telling about how the logs that went into building it came from a Negro church which had served as a place of worship for the local Negro community for over fifty years. Eventually, all the Negroes had moved away to other communities and the building was abandoned, so it was torn down and the materials went into building the Day house. Gramma seemed to view those old logs as evidence of being poor—poor but proud—and you could almost see the joy in her eyes when she spoke of the logs' origin.

Then there was the chimney, which Grampa envisioned as one of the most lasting accomplishments of his lifetime. Before obtaining a stove, they had cooked in the fireplace and it had provided warmth in the winter for all the years of their married life. Grampa occasionally had to mix some red clay with sagebrush straw from nearby fields to patch the cracks in the chimney caused by the weather and Father Time.

I also remembered the cracks in the walls and in the ceiling—where there *was* a ceiling. In some parts of the house, there was only that tin roof overhead. On dark nights, you could see a few stars through the nail holes in the tin, and every night, in the part of the house with a ceiling, you could hear the large wharf rats running across the ceiling joists. On the occasions when I'd caught a glimpse of those rats, I noticed that they always seemed to have an evil expression on their faces. I could imagine all sorts of bad things they could do to a person and I was afraid of them. But they never did anything but disappear when they spotted you, dragging their long tails in the musty dust that collected in the ceiling, and leaving a crooked trail I never had nerve enough to follow to their nesting place.

A huge mulberry tree was the lone survivor of the scene I was recalling. The sight of it brought with it the memory of my first really negative experience with Floyd—an experience that stuck with me through the years. It came back to me as I continued driving toward home, and though the memory was of a time twenty-plus years earlier, it was still fresh in my mind.

Five

June, 1951

I n 1951, I was not quite six years old but I was mean enough to be at least half grown, or so I had been told many times when I was on my worst behavior. (I was born September 17th, 1945 in an old log shack on a dirt road.)

It was a time of change for our whole family. Elizabeth, the oldest child, was out of high school and in New Orleans, working her way through nursing school. John R., the oldest of my brothers, had been in the Air Force for two years by then, having finished school and joined the service the year before Grampa's passing. In the summer of 1950, Billy Joe, who lacked one year of high school, also joined the Air Force. He had been terribly depressed his last year at home, between John R. being away in the service, and the death of his best friend, Grampa. All of us kids had loved Grampa very much, but none of us were as attached to him as Billy Joe. Popeye, at fourteen, was the oldest child left at home. Myra Lou was eleven, the twins, Ike and Mike, were nine, Gerald was nearing seven and Terry Gene was three.

This left me with four older brothers still at home, so, on occasion, I had to take my lumps. But, I was also known to give some, on a hit-and-run basis. And Terry Gene, bless his heart, was the only one little enough for me take anything out on. But, none of us boys really fought that much, no more so than most brothers. And Myra Lou got the respect she deserved—we didn't fight with her, and she didn't pick on us. Not too much, anyway.

During that summer, a man who worked with Floyd gave us a bicycle, but before we could ride it, the bike needed some new parts. The twins ordered the necessary parts from the Sears & Roebuck catalogue, and after waiting by the mailbox every day for nearly three weeks, the twins finally received the package.

I could hear their shouts of excitement as they left the mailbox out by the gravel road and headed for the front yard with that package. Blackie, the family milk cow, was lying near the gate, contentedly chewing her cud, when they came by her like twin whirlwinds. She lunged to get to her feet, but the effort was so great and her movement so slow, the twins were long gone before she even got halfway to her feet. She simply dropped back down and continued her chewing as if she had never been interrupted.

We had never had a bike before, so I was as excited as my brothers as I watched from the front porch of the house. It was quite a show, watching the twins tearing at the wrapping on the package. As he came into the yard, Ike called up to the porch. "Go find the tire pump so we can air the tires up!"

I immediately zipped out to the ragged, tin-covered shack we called our shop, in search of the pump. After five minutes of sorting through the blacksmith tools and the piles of assorted junk, I held up the pump triumphantly. By this time, the twins had the bike standing bottom side up in the shade of the mulberry tree, and were beginning to remove the parts that needed replacing.

Edra walked out onto the porch, intending to scold the boys for failing to eat the meal she had prepared for them. Instead, she ended up watching for a minute or two, and seeing how excited and busy her sons were, she decided to hold her tongue.

Gramma also watched us boys but, after a few minutes, she could see that the bicycle repair was going to take longer than we anticipated. She shouted to us, "You boys had better be worrying about hoein' that corn before Floyd comes in from work or y'all won't be able to even sit on the seat of that bicycle when he gets through with you!"

It wasn't unusual for Gramma to speak of Floyd with a touch of bitterness in her voice. She had witnessed so much of his abuse of Grampa, Edra, and us kids that it had placed this single flaw in this jewel of a woman who had sacrificed everything—her time, her money, her love, her entire existence to the care of us grandchildren.

Considering there were so many of us kids in the family, we needed two mothers to fully take care of us. And Gramma always seemed like a second mother instead of our grandmother, given that she and Edra shared all the motherly duties. Gramma was a tall, handsome woman with a pleasant and warm personality she had passed down to Edra, her tiny daughter who seemed to stop growing after she married Floyd and began having babies at fifteen years of age.

Gramma's warning certainly did speed up the progress on the bicycle repair project. None of us ever wanted to incur upon ourselves the wrath of Floyd's temper.

After much bickering over who was more mechanically inclined, and a couple of skinned knuckles, the twins got the new parts installed on the bike. Ike made a shaky trip out the front gate and down the gravel road about a hundred yards, with Mike yelling after him all the while, "Dammit, Ike, get back here and let me ride!"

Mike continued his yelling at Ike, and soon Popeye came out of the house and joined in the yelling. He wanted to ride the bike himself.

My brothers shared the bike until shortly before it was time for Floyd to arrive home from work. Then they went to the field to hoe the corn he had ordered them to hoe. I trailed along with them to the field, not planning to work, just to be where they were. Popeye and the twins knew that Floyd wouldn't check the field because it was Friday, Floyd's payday. That was the day he always brought a fifth of whiskey home with him, knowing he had the next two days off work. Floyd would ask them if they were finished with their work, only to hear them say they didn't quite get through but would finish in a short time on Saturday morning.

This day was one to be remembered for Ike and Mike because it was a day of much excitement in a time when things just weren't too exciting. In their minds, the last occasion to bring this much excitement to the household was much less pleasant. They were recalling a time when they were five years old.

They had been in the barn, playing with matches. Mike would hold a lighted match to the loose hay on the floor of the barn and let it burn for a short while, and then he'd get Ike to stamp it out. This worked fine until they switched roles. The problem was, Ike had shoes on and Mike didn't. When Ike lit the hay and asked Mike to stamp it out, he refused, for obvious reasons. They stood there arguing about it until it occurred to them that the fire was not waiting for them to settle the argument; it just refused to cooperate. By the time this became apparent to them, the hay was burning out of control, and the twins panicked. They ran to the woods behind the garden and hid there, hoping to avoid the whippings they were sure they would get.

This occurred while Grampa was still running the farm. By the time he finally noticed the fire, the barn was a total loss, as was the hay crop that had been stored there for the winter. And as far as the family knew, so were the twins, who had been seen entering the barn earlier.

The wailing of Edra and Gramma failed to bring the twins out of hiding right away. It never crossed the boys' minds that the family was grieving for them. The only thing they could think about was the punishment they were going to get, and they wanted to postpone it for as long as possible.

After the twins had been listening for a while to everyone desperately calling their names, they realized that the family was scared. They could hear them shouting to one another that the boys must have been trapped in the loft of the barn and burned to death. Realizing the family's fear of their death was more important than protecting their hides, the two emerged from hiding, ready to take their punishment.

When the boys came sneaking around the back fence of the garden and Edra spotted them, she ran to them crying and hugged them both together, followed by Gramma who did the same. The twins were slightly perplexed by this reaction, as they expected everyone to be mad at them. Grampa's reaction when he got his hands on them later was something they understood perfectly. Grampa gave the boys a spanking, but he did so without anger; the only part of the affair that evoked emotion in him once he'd realized the boys were safe was his realization that the following winter was going to be harder than most, after losing his hay crop and his barn. He could not afford to replace either of them.

When Floyd did arrive home from work that Friday afternoon, the bike stood idle in the yard and all us boys were still out in the cornfield, where we lingered until we were sure it was alright to stop for the day. We knew when Floyd did not come out to check on us that he was beyond the point of really caring whether the corn was hoed or not.

Walking into the house, we knew we had figured right because Floyd was in a good mood. "You boys get to bed early tonight 'cause we're goin' fishin' in the mornin'."

Floyd's promise brought smiles from them all. We didn't get to go fishing nearly as often as we would have liked, and now we had an enjoyable time to look forward to the next day.

The whiskey was always there, a sometimes pleasant but usually unpleasant, part of our lives. For the most part, and in most situations, the rest of the family had become adept at coping with it. At this point in time, Terry Gene and I were the only children in the family who had not yet learned to read Floyd's moods when he'd been drinking. We were still too young. It seemed the only time he ever showed any signs of caring for us was sometimes when he had been drinking. Then, he would laugh and joke with us and, from time to time, give us a quarter each, which we would spend on candy and Cokes at Uncle Clayton Day's commissary by the abandoned sawmill down the road. At other times, the whiskey turned him into a sour, mean person who would take his razor strap to any of us who, in his viewpoint, stepped out of line.

Early in life, I had learned to respect and fear that razor strap. Sometimes when I was alone in the house, I would take it down from the nail on the wall where it hung, and stand by the rickety table with the wash basin on it, rubbing my fingers across the slick surface of the leather, wondering how in the world such smooth leather could put the razor edge on a piece of steel. But, mostly, I would be reminded to avoid doing anything while Floyd was around that might cause him to use the strap on me. I had seen what it could do!

The next morning came alive with the birds singing in the trees surrounding the house. And, in the early morning sunlight, the dew was glistening on all the flowers and shrubs that Edra had so carefully nurtured in the yard.

My brothers and I were sleeping three to a bed when Floyd came in that morning and made a pass between the two beds. He roughly shook us awake, instructing us to get out and dig some worms and get our fishing poles together. "We ought to be fishin' already!" he said.

I was the first one to hit the floor because I wanted a bite to eat before I did anything, especially before digging around looking for a bunch of slimy earthworms in that worm bed filled with cow manure. As soon as I pulled my clothes on, I went into the kitchen and poured some ribbon cane syrup into a saucer, and began mopping it up with a hot biscuit, dripping some of it on my chin. I wiped most of it off, but I missed enough to attract an entire day's worth of dirt. This spot would be a dark blotch on my face by suppertime even though it was hardly noticeable at that moment.

Having quickly devoured that one biscuit, I ran out the back door to join the others at the worm bed, a wooden frame placed on the ground under the mulberry tree where it could stay cool and damp. This frame was partially filled with dirt, but mostly it was filled with dried cow manure. Floyd had put a handful of red wigglers in this mixture, and once a week he sprinkled some cornmeal, used coffee grounds, and water over it to produce an abundance of the little red worms over the period of a few months. This seemed an unlikely diet for anything, but the worms seemed to thrive on it.

"Ike, I wish you would hurry up!" Mike fussed. "I'm findin' two to your one!"

"Aw, shut up!" Ike retorted. "I'm just pickin' out the biggest and the best!" It wouldn't have been a normal day if the twins had not begun it by arguing.

"Both of y'all shut up and just dig for worms," Pop-eye instructed. Since he was the oldest brother present, he was the man in charge. The voice of authority was always the older brother when there were only us boys present; except, that is, when the twins were the oldest present. They could never agree on who would be boss and many times this led to a fight between them.

Popeye decided we had enough worms as he raised the can toward the ray of sunlight peeping over his shoulder and inspected the mass of squirming red wig-glers all in a tangled wad at the bottom of the can. He scooped up some dirt from the worm bed with his hands and dropped it into the can.

Heading for the truck, Popeye told the twins, "Ike, you go get the fishin' poles and Mike, you go get a jug of water."

"I'll go get a tote sack!" I volunteered, and ran for the back of the potato house where the burlap feed sacks were stored for use when digging potatoes. On this par-ticular day, one would be used to drop the fish into as they were caught. Then the top of the sack would be hooked securely under a root on the creek bank and the bottom would hang down into the creek. This would keep the fish fresh and alive; they would still be jumping when we returned home with them.

All of us boys were in the faded, green Ford truck when Floyd came out of the house after a breakfast of salt bacon and eggs. I was alone in the cab of the truck, while Popeye, Gerald and the twins had piled into the rear of the truck, sitting alongside the fishing gear. Terry Gene was still in bed, having gone back to sleep in pretty much the same instant he had been awakened.

I had by then grown used to hearing of the distrust my older brothers had for Floyd, but I was not yet fully aware of the difference between their attitudes toward him and mine. I would later recognize the significance of time and its bearing on our individual feelings toward our father. As we grew older and saw more of the meaner side of Floyd, we would grow to dislike him more deeply as both a father and a person. In later years, I would often wonder how different each of us might have been if the innocence of our youth had been left unscarred by the brutalities that took it away.

On the morning of that fishing trip as I sat in the cab of the truck, I was thoroughly happy, my innocence was intact, and I was oblivious to my brothers' conflicted feelings about going fishing. I was still too young to understand how they could be anticipating the fishing trip with as much excitement and happiness as I was, and yet also be uneasy leaving home with Floyd, knowing that he would be drinking, and therefore unpredictable, while they were fishing.

Around the time I was born, my older siblings' allegiance to Floyd had begun to fade at an accelerated rate. They had each witnessed Floyd being mean to Grampa and hateful to Edra and Gramma, especially when he was drinking. They all harbored feelings of distrust toward Floyd, and maybe even hatred, and these emotions were expressed around us younger kids. Gramma, too, voiced her dislike of Floyd, and this influenced all of us in our thinking as we grew older.

I was the ninth child on the scene, with Gerald only one year older, and the twins—Ike and Mike—only four and small for their age. By that point in time, the strain on Edra and Gramma had become too much. They had their hands full with such a large family, between feeding everyone, keeping all of us in clean clothing, looking after the house, and taking care of four small children. It caused so much strain, in fact, that Gerald was farmed out to Uncle Walter and Aunt Ruth for about seven months.

I could only imagine what a confusing period this must have been for both Gerald and my other siblings. It was a drastic change in atmosphere for Gerald when he left home, but the change he faced upon his return was even greater, for he had been spoiled by Aunt Ruth, and then dumped back into the confusion of Franklin daily family life.

Aunt Ruth had been a very doting foster mother, dressing Gerald in suits, occasionally taking him into the nearby town of Marion, and spoiling him in general, while just across the forty-acre cotton field, the rest of his brothers and sisters were resigned to the daily hardship to which they were accustomed. We were a bit jealous, but we were also happy for Gerald.

It seemed to be a long way to the Polly Dean Hole, the best fishing hole on the creek, but it was actually only about four miles. The old truck and the winding, pot-hole-filled dirt road did make it rather a lengthy trip, but at last we came to the steep hill which crested just above the creek, and our favorite fishing spot could be seen to the left of the road, at the bottom of the long hill.

As the truck came to a halt at the bottom of the hill, there was a mad scramble for the fishing poles and the worms. We each wanted to be the one to catch the first fish, this feat being a trophy of sorts in the mind of the lucky one. We unrolled our lines which had been wound around the length of the poles like a stripe around a bar-ber's pole, baited our hooks, and lined the creek bank with great anticipation.

We hadn't been fishing more than a couple of min-utes when Ike began yelling, "I got one!" He jerked his cane pole upwards with a goggle-eye fish the size of his hand dangling from the line. Ike was all smiles.

The goggle-eye was a cross between the creek trout and a bream. It took on the features of each fish about equally. They never seemed to get very big but they were really good fighters and were delicious when fried good and crisp.

The rest of us boys were envious of Ike, but we didn't let ourselves stay distracted for long from our own corks which would indicate the slightest bump of the hook by a fish. We didn't have to wait long because the creek was at its lowest level of the year and fishing was good.

Floyd watched us for a few minutes and then he began gathering wood for a fire. That morning, he had talked about cleaning and cooking the fish while we were down by the creek, and he had brought along a cardboard box containing grease, cornmeal, and a frying pan, along with other necessities for a cookout.

Once he had gathered enough wood and started the fire, Floyd sat down by a large oak tree, gazing into the fire and occasionally taking a drink from the fifth of whiskey. About half an hour later, he dozed off for a few minutes and when he awakened, he started yelling at us boys to get ready to go home. It seemed he had completely forgotten about cooking our catch down by the creek.

All of us boys were disappointed and started grumbling, but we took care to keep the volume low enough that Floyd wouldn't hear us. None of us wanted to take a severe scolding or worse for complaining to him or begging to stay longer. We just gathered together our poles and fish and headed for the truck, piling into the rear. This time, I climbed in the rear of the truck with the others. I felt guilty about not riding up front with Floyd, but I would have felt even more guilty had I failed to join my brothers in their closeted protests over getting our fishing trip cut short just when we were really beginning to enjoy it.

Floyd turned the key in the ignition and began the climb up the hill, which was almost too steep for the truck, its power diminished by eighty thousand miles of use at the hands of some other owner before Floyd. At first, us five boys were leaning excitedly over the sides of the pickup bed, and watching the tires spin as the vehicle strained against the hard climb. Then my brothers resumed their fussing about Floyd, irritated that he didn't seem to care that he had interrupted our fun.

"He always does us this way," said Popeye. "All he wanted to come down here for was so he could drink his whiskey in peace. Y'all watch and see, he'll probably hit the ditch before we make it home 'cause he's had over half that jug!"

"Yeah, he's already staggerin'," noted Mike, as he looked at Ike. They nodded their heads in unison.

I only watched and listened, trying hard to stay neutral. I was confused because I didn't really see that much reason to complain. We had caught a good many fish and enjoyed it while it lasted. At five years old, I couldn't quite comprehend why my older brothers were as bitter as they were toward Floyd.

Only years later would I come to understand what made Floyd the way he was and what made us boys the way we were. (I hoped that, in time, my siblings would come to understand, as well.) Floyd drank because he had to, I supposed. He did work hard and made us work in order to keep ourselves fed. That alone was a major accomplishment, considering the size of our family.

Later that same day, I would be given my first dose of the medicine that my older brothers and sisters had been swallowing for years.

We were all quiet when we arrived home. We went at once to the back porch where we spread out the fish on some boards and began scaling them with spoons Edra handed us from the kitchen. Popeye got out his pocket knife to finish cleaning the fish after us younger boys had scraped off the scales, and he was completely in charge of the catfish, which had to be skinned with pliers, a task which took more muscle and experience than the twins or I had. I wasn't getting all the scales off the fish I scraped, so I had all my brothers fussing at me. I was rescued from that slimy operation by my inexperience and lack of attention to detail, and away I ran, looking for a more pleasant way to spend my time.

Floyd had taken a pillow and a blanket out to the mulberry tree and spread them out so he could lay down in the shade where it was a little cooler than in the sultry confines of the tin-roofed house. He liked to do this when he had a bottle to finish. He would intermittently doze and read a Zane Grey western novel while occasionally taking another shot of whiskey, which was usually followed by a cigarette which he rolled from the can of Prince Albert tobacco he carried in the bib of his overalls.

After removing my shoes, which I had been wearing to protect my feet from any hostile water moccasins during the fishing trip, and the shirt I'd worn to ward off the mosquitoes, I ran out the front door of the house and jumped off the porch, which was almost four feet from the ground and looked about twice that far to me. I took advantage of the freedom afforded me by the twins' absorption in their fish-cleaning task, and took the bike from the spot where it had been parked the previous evening.

I was too small to even think about riding it, so I grasped the seat with my right hand, the handlebar with my left, and began pushing it around the perimeter of the house. There was just barely enough space in many places for the bike to pass between the house and various trees and bushes Edra had planted, such as the fig tree near the back porch and the pomegranate by the chimney which was built from the ground up outside the house, and attached to the wall.

After a couple of trips around the outside of the house, I felt like a pro maneuvering the bike through this treacherous course. I found that I could steer the bike by simply leaning it in the direction I wanted it to go, so I removed my hand from the handlebar. I was in a world all my own as I rounded the front corner of the house with the bike leaned over so far toward myself that I could see over the top of it.

As I began to straighten it up, the front wheel struck a four-inch-deep hole scratched out in the dirt by Spot, the spotted cur which each of us boys claimed as our own. I had steered the bike around this hole before, but with my slightly unsteady method of steering without holding onto the handlebar, I was unable to avoid the hole on this particular trip.

In trying to correct the erratic course caused by the front wheel falling into the hole, I over-corrected and the sudden shifting of the bike's weight caused me to completely lose control of it. Though I fought in vain to bring it back under control, my efforts were fruitless as the bike covered, in a wobbly trail, the fifteen feet to where Floyd lay in a half-asleep stupor. I felt an impending sense of doom as the bike ungraciously dumped itself in a pile of spinning wheels and pedal bolts naked of pedals right on top of Floyd. And to add insult to injury, my over-anxious efforts to keep this very thing from happening resulted in me losing my balance and falling on top of the whole mess.

It didn't take me long to scramble up from there, and as soon as I did, I grabbed the bike and tried to lift it. But it was too heavy for me, and I just made matters worse by dropping it right back onto Floyd.

Floyd grunted when first hit and woke up cursing and flailing his arms, a wild look in his eyes. He threw the bike off himself and as he stood up, the cursing he was directing my way took on an added intensity. His eyes were afire with the madness that was so familiar to the rest of the family, but I noticed it then for the first time in my life, and it was frightening.

I could feel my face blush and as I ducked my head, staring at the ground, not knowing what to do, Floyd grabbed my arm and began dragging me across the yard to the big, bushy grapevine near the back porch. Then he pulled out his pocket knife, and opened the blade with his teeth, all the while holding me by my arm as if he were afraid I would run away. Then, he reached down and cut a vine half an inch in diameter, stripped the leaves from three feet of the vine, and placing his foot on the loose end, cut this off with an upward thrust of the knife.

Placing the knife back in the pocket of his overalls, Floyd picked up the rough, knotty vine and, still cursing, began to beat me violently across my bare back, the blows ranging from near my neck down to my knees.

It was to be possibly the only time in my life that I was totally terrified, to the point where I was nearly in a daze. As I writhed in the awful, cutting pain, I tried to scream but I could only make a weak, gasping sound as the blows kept raining down on my back, bringing blood in a series of dots, connected by dark red lines across my back where the knots in the vine struck me.

The beating continued for several minutes and, totally panicked, I wondered what had happened to my voice. Why couldn't I make any sound other than that pitiful, whispered whine? The pain suddenly began to subside, my breathing stopped, and then everything stopped working. I slipped into unconsciousness, no longer able to feel anything.

I can only imagine how terrified Edra must have been as she ran over to us, crying out and begging Floyd to stop beating me. He stopped only long enough to push her away violently, causing her to fall backwards to the ground, stunned by the jolt and also by the knowledge that she could only sit there and helplessly watch. She screamed as she saw the shock and pain that had stolen my breath away.

Popeye had watched, frozen in fright, with a sickening feeling in his stomach, unable to move until Edra's scream brought him back to life. He knew that something had to be done and it had to be done at once!

He ran across the yard and grabbed Floyd from behind, hurling him in a spinning motion away from me. Floyd fell to the ground in an exhausted heap, cursing and threatening Popeye, who ignored him as he picked me up and started for the porch at the rear of the house. My breathing had not resumed and my face was beginning to turn a ghostly shade of blue.

My brothers and sisters, along with Gramma, had been watching in horror as this scene unfolded. As Popeye passed them on his way into the house, they were all afraid to come too close, fearing the worst when they saw the color of my face.

Realizing I was still not breathing, Popeye shook my body violently, holding me out in front of him. Looking into my face, which looked unreal in its dark, lifeless condition, he said, "Come on, Freddy Ray, breathe! Breathe! Do you hear me? Breathe!"

Edra had caught up with Popeye by this time, and as my brother stood on the back porch of the house, shaking me, she laid her left hand on Popeye's shoulder and pulled me toward herself with her right arm. As she took me from Popeye's grasp, my body arched and then stiffened suddenly.

There was a loud gasp and my body relaxed completely. It was the moment of truth, and neither Edra nor Popeye knew exactly what it meant—until I began sobbing. Then they knew. No one could ever know the sensation of joy that swept over Edra when she heard the sound of my scared crying.

Mother Nature has been known to take care of things in ways that we cannot understand, I suppose, and this had been her way of eliminating the brunt of the pain and blocking from my mind and memory most of that awful event.

As Edra reached the bedroom and my bed, we were both breathing a lot easier. She gently eased me down onto the bed, and she and Popeye watched the color of my face rapidly return to normal. Gramma, along with the rest of the kids, crowded through the door, peering at me. All was quiet except for my sobbing, which was getting quieter now.

Edra sat on the edge of the bed and held my hand as she kissed me, wanting to turn me over to where she could see my back, and yet not wanting to. Looking up, I saw all the concerned faces gazing down at me and I began to feel a lot better. The burning sensation of the cuts on my back began to fade, but the blood continued to ooze and soak onto the sheet.

I closed my eyes and began to drift off to sleep. Edra decided to wait until after I awakened before inspecting the cuts on my back. Then she would put some kerosene on my wounds, tear some strips from an old sheet, and wrap those around me. As my mother lay there consoling me and tending to my wounds, I'm sure she was recalling a similar incident that had taken place about twelve years prior, when Billy Joe suffered a beating at the hands of Floyd. I can only assume that she wondered then, *How many more times will my children have to endure this type of treatment?*

At the time of his beating, Billy Joe was not much older than I was at the time of my whipping. As my brother recalled the event many years later, he told of feeling the blood running down the back sides of his legs after being whipped so viciously. Neither Billy Joe, nor John R. who witnessed it, could remember Floyd's reason for whipping him.

Six

Six weeks after the beating I had taken, my visible wounds were healed and I had almost forgotten the whole affair. Little did I know at the time that the beating was to become the first piece in a jigsaw puzzle that would assemble itself over the next couple of years, showing me the complete picture.

For the Fourth of July, there was a large gathering of relatives at the farm, including my cousin, Bryan Carpenter, and his family. They visited us every summer, driving all the way from the western part of Texas, which might as well have been the other side of the world, as far as I was concerned.

Whenever Bryan was around, I had to be constantly on guard. He liked to see if he could playfully slap or pinch me before I saw him coming, and I enjoyed the challenge of anticipating when he was about to try something and dodging quickly enough to keep him from being successful with his mischief. My cousin was two years older and seemed to delight in teasing me, but we admired each other because we were both strong for our age, and always showing off our prowess in foot races, high jumps, and any other activity that required athletic ability.

The Fourth of July celebration was enjoyed immensely by everyone, and our whole family hated to see our Texas relatives' visit come to an end. The time we spent together was the high point of our summer. We kids were always stuck out in the country with nowhere to go and nothing to do but entertain ourselves any way we could.

During the summertime, the only connection we had with the rest of the world came from the radio Floyd kept in his little bedroom which had been framed up from part of the original front porch. Aside from the radio, about the only thing left for us were our farm chores, made even more unpleasant than usual by the hot, humid summer weather. That week in particular had been no exception, and all of us boys were looking forward to a break on Saturday afternoon.

Ike and Mike left home shortly after the midday meal to visit with their friends, Huey and Dewey Rhodes, who lived at the Alabama Landing on the Ouachita River. Ike and Mike and the Rhodes twins were the same age, and they spent as much time together as possible.

Mr. Rhodes was a fisherman, and he only raised a small garden by their house near the river, which meant that Huey and Dewey had fewer chores than Ike and Mike, and a little more spare time. On that particular day, they had finished helping their dad at the boat landing and were headed for our house, which was about two miles up the gravel road from the river.

The two sets of twins met around the halfway point, and turned back toward our farm, walking the dusty road and trading criticisms. Ike and Mike had always jokingly criticized each other, and the Rhodes twins did the same, but if anyone else tried it, the twins would team up on them. If you criticized either twin, you would suffer the wrath of both.

As they neared the farm, they left the road and sat down under some sweet gum saplings growing in a grove near the road. Their conversation eventually led to making bets about which of them could ride down the largest sapling. Sweet gum trees in the sapling stage are very limber, and the boys delighted in climbing to the top of them. Once at the top, they would sway back and forth until they could swing their body away from the trunk of the tree, causing it to bend over in a U-shaped arch until their feet touched the ground. The sapling would shoot upwards when they released their grip on it, switching back and forth among the treetops for a moment, slightly bowed like the others that had been conquered in the same fashion.

After Dewey (who was a bit on the heavy side, giving him a slight advantage) established himself as the champ, they sat down to have a short rest and talk about what else they could do to entertain themselves. As Ike lay with his head on a root, gazing upwards through the treetops, he suddenly thought of a way they could ride down a much taller sapling than Dewey's prizewinner. Two or three of the boys could climb one tree and the added weight would ride down a real prize.

They all jumped up, agreeing and smiling in anticipation of what might happen. Would a larger sapling snap under the strain? Or would they get it leaned over halfway only to have it stop, leaving them to drop to the ground? This happened sometimes, but with a smaller sapling, the drop to the ground was never more than four or five feet. The taller sapling, on the other hand, could result in a drop of maybe ten to fifteen feet, dangerous by any measure. They were all tough and accustomed to taking hard knocks, so there was little apprehension in their minds at all.

"Hey, I'll tell y'all what we ought to do," Mike said. "Let's go get a rope and we'll tie the sapling down to the bottom of another sweet gum after we ride it down. Then one of us can get on and ride it back up when we cut the rope. I'll bet that would be a humdinger of a ride!"

The other three boys agreed with Mike and sent him to the barn to get a rope.

I had a calf by the tail at the moment Mike entered the barnyard, and I was running around the perimeter of the barnyard fence, generally having a ball and scaring the poor calf half to death. A calf didn't have a chance for much peace on our farm. We Franklin boys were prone to subject it to various forms of rugged recreation, such as being bulldogged, roped or ridden like a rodeo bull.

Mike had been thinking that he didn't really want to be the guinea pig in their plan to ride the big sapling, and when he spotted me, he suddenly found the answer to his problem. "Hey, Freddy Ray! Come go with me. We're riding down sweet gum saplings and we need your help."

The twins didn't like having me hang around when they had company, so I should have known that something was up when Mike invited me to join them. I liked to be with my older brothers, especially when the Rhodes twins were around, so I joined Mike, who was running from the barn with a short rope in his hands. My departure brought instant relief for the frightened calf.

Together we sprinted down the gravel road toward the grove of sweet gum trees. Even though we were both barefoot, the gravel in the road didn't bother us at all. We'd been going barefoot since spring, and by then, our bare feet were as tough as shoe leather.

As Mike and I left the road and entered the grove, Ike and the Rhodes twins were already climbing one of the tallest sweet gum trees. They yelled for Mike to join them when they saw us approaching. So, he handed me the rope and started up the tree to join the others.

I watched them work their way through the limbs until they got near the top where they all huddled as close together as they could. I could see enough to tell that Mike was whispering something to the others, and I saw them nod their heads and grin, but I gave little thought to what Mike might have been saying. The boys started to sway back and forth together until the tree began to lean toward the ground more with each effort. I judged the distance the tree would extend when arched over, and took a few steps backwards so I'd be clear of it when it swung to the ground.

"Ride him, cowboys!" I yelled to them, and in response they began to whoop and yell.

And ride him, they did. The sapling arched down slowly until Huey, who was closer to the top, touched the ground with the tips of his toes. They continued to pull and swing until the others had their feet on the ground, and then they tied the rope around the base of a nearby tree and then around the downed sapling.

"Come on, Freddy Ray, you're the one who needs to ride it back up when we cut the rope," Mike said, grabbing me by the arm and leading me over to the tree.

Now I knew why I had been invited to join them. I figured out right away that Mike was scared to ride the tree when they cut it loose, and he'd seen a potential test pilot when he spotted me with the calf. The other boys all agreed that, because of my size, I ought to be the one to make the ride.

I was just dumb enough and brave enough to agree to do what they asked, so I climbed aboard, almost standing on my head as I wrapped my arms and legs around the sapling close to the top where it was tied. After I agreed to do this, and before the rope was cut, I realized I was going to be really high up in the air when the sapling flew back up. I tried to fake a look of confidence as I prepared for the blastoff, but I was apprehensive and a little bit afraid. Since I didn't see any way out of it without appearing to be chicken, I made up my mind to hang on tight and enjoy the ride.

Mike was now beginning to wonder if he had been wise in even suggesting that I be the rider. He apprehensively approached the end of the rope at the base of the tree where it was tied. "Now, Freddy Ray, you hold on tight, 'cause this thing is liable to shoot back up fast!" he said, reaching up and patting me on the back. Then he kneeled down and began trying to cut the rope with the dull little pocketknife he produced from the front pocket of his jeans. The knife had seen better days, and now it had to be pulled back and forth across the rope at least a dozen times before it sliced completely through.

Mike had forced a smile upon his face before. But his smile quickly faded and turned into a worried expression as he watched the sweet gum make its swift ascent, swishing past its upright position into a downward arch on the opposite side, which ended its descent and began its return ascent in a split second. The sudden change of direction placed such tremendous force against my grip that I could no longer hold my feet together, and my legs were thrown straight out from the trunk of the tree. I was really frightened now, and tightened my grip on the tree, barely managing to keep from being shot outwards like a rock from a catapult.

My weight finally equalized with the switching top, but not before the treetop went switching back and forth in a jarring motion, bruising my legs from top to bottom in short spurts as they beat against the rough bark.

By the time the tree came to complete stillness save for the fluttering of a few leaves, I was in a weakened state. I gingerly lowered myself to the nearest point where my feet would rest on a limb, and bear-hugged the tree trunk, fighting against the tears that wanted to come from the fright and pain of this near disaster. I held onto the tree until I regained my composure.

Satisfied that I was safe, Mike looked at the others on the ground around the sapling, and smiled, "Did y'all see his eyes bug out?" He shouted it loudly enough to make sure I heard him. The other three boys laughed loudly.

As I began to climb down through the branches, I could hear the others laughing and joking about me.

"Yeah, I think he'll have to go home and change his britches, too!" said Huey, loudly, and the laughter among the boys grew even louder.

Dropping from the lowest limb onto the ground, I only grinned, with a cocky expression on my face. Looking them over scornfully, I piped up, "Y'all are just chicken shit! Too damned scared to ride it yourselves!" I had heard the older boys talk that way often enough in the past when they were away from any of the grownups, and now I felt as if I had earned the right to do the same.

"Boy, I'll make you think chicken!" Ike said, running toward me and unbuckling his belt as if he planned to whip me with it.

Like a flash, I was off and running at full speed, darting around trees, first to my left and then to my right. Ike was no match for me in a foot race that required more agility than speed, so after a short distance, he yelled to me, "I'll catch you when you're not expecting it and I'll tear your little butt up!"

I only laughed as I looked back over my shoulder, settling down to a trot and continuing toward the barnyard where I could finish tiring out the calf so I could bulldog him. As I entered the barnyard, my legs were still aching and I realized just how thirsty I was, so I ran over to the backyard fence, zigzagging from the pasture to the garden, and vaulted over the fence. Then I ran to the back porch where I stepped up on the oak tree stump which had been cut and placed there for a step. I grabbed the long-handled metal dipper out of the water pail hanging on a nail in a post supporting the back porch. The pail rattled, which meant I would have to draw water from the well if I were going to have a drink.

I unhooked the bail of the bucket from the nail and carried it the thirty feet to the well, then placed it on the ground beside the square well curb that had been formed from cypress lumber and placed in the well as it had been dug. I untied the rope from the A-frame over the well and removed the lid from the well curb. The lid was a lard-bucket lid, and it covered the opening almost completely so as to keep any debris from falling into the well.

As I guided the long, narrow well bucket down the curb, the rope coiled around my feet began to disappear up over the well pulley and down into the well. I heard the bucket splash into the water at the same instant the rope stopped uncoiling. After hesitating a moment, the bucket slowly sank into the water and became heavy on the end of the rope. I began pulling the rope back through the pulley, which squeaked from the lack of oil, along with the squeaking of the wooden A-frame and the rusty haywire with which the pulley was tied. It was almost too much of a load for me, and I grumbled as the bucket's bottom cleared the top of the curb.

I pushed it over to rest on the curb for a moment, and then swung it over the bucket on the ground, hooked my thumb in the ring at the top of the well bucket, and released the water in a long, refreshing look-ing splash. I drank my fill of the cool water and then returned the water bucket to the post on the back porch. It took a mighty effort on my part to lift the bucket high enough to hook the bail on the nail, but I managed to do so, though I sloshed some of the water out while trying.

As I jumped from the porch, Floyd came out the back door with a plate full of dinner scraps in his hand and called to me. I turned and as I did, Floyd stepped down from the porch and shoved the plate of scraps into my hands, causing the pot liquor (the water and juice from cooking the vegetables) to splash over the edge of the plate and run down my arms, dripping off my elbows.

"Here, call that damned spotted dog out yonder in the field!" Floyd said. "I caught that son of a bitch in the hen house a while ago, robbing a nest, and I ain't gonna have no damned egg-suckin' dog around here!"

My heart sank as I realized what this meant, and now I wished I had stayed away longer. I trembled as I went through the back gate which led into the field and called for Spot. I had spent many happy hours rambling through the nearby fields and woods with Spot, and now I was being forced to lead to his death this dog who would not come out of hiding for Floyd.

A lump came to my throat when I saw Spot cautiously step out of some tall weeds and peer around until he was sure it was safe to come out. The kick in the ribs Spot had received as he made his escape from the hen house had made him wary but he eagerly ran to me when he saw the plate of scraps I was holding.

My brothers and I were very attached to Spot, even though he was not very useful. He had never learned to hunt, but he loved to be petted and was so playful, you couldn't help liking him. Only Floyd had managed to remain indifferent to the dog's charms. He didn't have any use for the dog because he wouldn't hunt, and he didn't think a dog was worth feeding unless he could help put some meat in the pot. But the fact that the family was so poor, and had very few scraps to feed the dogs, was the very thing that led the hungry dog to the eggs in the hen house.

I knew I was leading Spot to his death and I also knew I had no choice, recalling the beating I had received earlier in the summer. I wanted so badly to beg Floyd not to kill the dog, but my fear of my father was too much. So, I just hung my head in sorrow as I saw Floyd come out of the house with a .22 rifle in his hand and sit down on the porch with his feet resting on the step.

He motioned for me to move away, and as soon as I was out of the line of fire, he raised the rifle to his shoulder and aimed at Spot, who was eating hungrily, oblivious to everything around him. I began feeling sick to my stomach, and my mouth became so dry, I felt as though I had not had any water for hours. I was startled when I heard the shot ring out because I was still close to the dog, and I didn't expect Floyd to shoot with me so nearby.

I watched in horror as Spot dropped in his tracks, his head falling straight down and coming to rest in the plate of food he had just been enjoying. Blood flowed from the bullet hole directly between his eyes, and overflowed from the plate as it filled.

It was quick, it was sickening, and it was everything I could do to keep from vomiting. The incident became permanently etched into my five-year-old mind, deepening my awareness of the cruel side of Floyd as I witnessed it being manifested once again.

"God dammit, boy! Can't you hear?" Floyd shouted. "I told you to go drag that bastard off down yonder to them woods!"

I had not heard these instructions the first time, and now they jarred me temporarily from my shock. I started for the shop building where I found an old piece of rope. Then I headed out to the place where my fallen friend lay, and beheld the most horrible, saddening sight I had witnessed in my short life.

The two sets of twins were drawn to the house by the sound of the rifle, and appeared beside me now. I stood there in tears, helpless—I was too small to pick up Spot and carry him, and couldn't bear to touch him to tie the rope around his legs so I could drag him away.

"What happened?" Mike asked, not wanting to believe what he saw.

"Floyd caught him in the hen house and he just killed him," I mumbled, shaking my head slowly from side to side.

Ike took the rope from my hands and knelt down by Spot. He hesitated for a moment, and then stood up and ran toward the barn, quickly returning with an old woolen blanket, ordinarily used as a saddle blanket. He spread this on the ground and motioned for the others to help place the dog's body on it. After they managed to get Spot onto the blanket, they each gathered up a corner of the blanket to pick it up and, with their heads bowed, began walking slowly toward the back of the pasture, with me trailing along behind them.

"We've got to dig a grave and bury him," Ike said. "We can't just leave him for the buzzards. Under the plum tree will be a good restin' place." He pointed to the old gnarled tree standing alone near the back pasture fence.

"Yeah, that's a real good place," agreed Mike, as they veered to the left and carried Spot the remaining few yards to his final resting place. After reaching the shade of the plum tree and laying their burden down, Mike ran to the barn to fetch the shovel.

In a matter of only twenty minutes, the two sets of twins had the grave dug, each taking a turn on the shovel. They carefully wrapped the ragged blanket around Spot and, getting down on their knees, lowered him into the grave. Ike pulled off the faded green baseball cap he was wearing and placed it over his heart. "Lord, may he rest in peace," he solemnly prayed. "He was a good dog."

The other boys, with their heads bowed, followed with an "Amen."

"Why did he have to kill him?" I asked, staring down at the blanket-wrapped form. "He could have whipped him and made him stay out of the hen house. That's all he would'a had to do!"

Mike, still on his knees beside the grave, began slowly raking dirt into it with his hands, with the others following suit. After several moments of silence, he stopped raking the dirt and leaned back on his heels, looking up at me where I stood watching with a sad look on my face. I knew he could tell that I was trying to keep from crying.

He stood up and placed his arm around my shoulder. "You need to be a little man, Freddy Ray, 'cause Floyd, he just don't give a damn."

I thought I understood why Mike said what he did, and I silently vowed that it would take a lot more than that to make me cry in the future.

Seven

September, 1951

The first of September began a completely new chapter in my life, as I entered the first grade at Linville School.

I was amazed and just a wee bit bewildered by all I encountered there. For starters, as the first day of school began with a bus trip over a route I had never completely traveled, I noticed that most people lived in houses that looked more modern than my family's house. The only one I saw that looked worse than ours was on the edge of a cotton field on a little narrow dirt road. The tin roof on the house was so rusty, it looked as if it were a hundred years old.

In a field across the road from the house, I saw an old bearded man, along with some Negroes, picking cotton. Or maybe the man wasn't all that old, but his long, gray beard gave me that impression. I didn't remember ever seeing a man with a beard before that day.

Standing on the front porch of the house was a frail looking old woman in ragged clothes. She was a sister to the man who owned the farm, and as far as anyone seemed to know, she had not been off the farm in years. As the school bus approached the front of the house, she turned and quickly stepped through the door.

The whole scene stirred my imagination, and I strained my eyes to see as much as I could of it as the bus drove by. In the years to come, I would remain fascinated with the place and the people who lived there, and I would one day learn more about them than I could through the school bus window. Even though the opinions I formed of this twosome during that time were formed from a distance, I would learn later in life that they were extremely accurate.

The brother, Mac Pace, was an honest, hard-working man, who asked no one for help. He raised most of his food there on the farm, and he and his sister needed little beyond that—only flour and sugar and such. As for clothing, they made their simple wardrobe last beyond its typical life. Mac's sister was also a hard worker, a sweet woman who could neither face life outside her home nor desired it.

Further down the road, I saw a house painted white, with a picket fence and a mowed lawn surrounding it, and I wished to someday have a house just like it. At our house, the yard had to withstand the constant traffic of boys, dogs, and chickens, so the grass had little chance to grow. Instead of mowing the yard, we swept it with a switch-cane broom.

By the time I arrived at school, I had a brand new awareness that most families seemed a bit more successful than my own. But I was wearing a new pair of shoes and a new pair of blue jeans together for the first time in my life, and I felt pretty good about that. Before that day, I had always had nothing but hand-me-downs from a procession of older brothers.

After our arrival at Linville School, my sister, Myra Lou, following Edra's instructions, directed me to the first grade and introduced me to my teacher. Mrs. Green welcomed me and then pointed toward the playground, telling me that I could go play until the bell rang, at which time I was to return to the classroom to begin the school day.

As I approached the playground, I saw several boys my age playing there, and about half of them were wearing short pants. Edra had tried to get me to wear short pants but I had refused with such stubbornness, she finally gave up trying.

"I ain't wearin' no sissy pants!" I had told her, in no uncertain terms. I followed with a few select cusswords, knowing I could get away with such talk with her.

"You're as stubborn as any mule there ever was," she told me. She had already found that, of the eight of us boys she had at this point, I was the most stubborn of the bunch.

As I looked around at the other first graders, I thought about my argument with Edra. I was glad I had stood my ground because the boys with short britches sure did look like sissies to me. *I could whup any of them little momma's boys,* I thought to myself.

Fighting had been for me an almost-every-day affair, being the seventh son and the target of all the older brothers at one time or another. This was mainly because I was always provoking them and alternately fighting gamely or being swift to retreat to a safe distance. The first day of school opened up a whole new world to me, and I couldn't wait to show the other boys in my class who was the toughest, and who could run the fastest. It was going to be a lot of fun!

Time flew by quickly over the next few weeks as I settled into the routine of school and made it known that I was tough for a first grader. I whipped or bluffed all the first grade boys, except those I liked, which wasn't too hard since there were only about a half-dozen boys in the first grade. I fought several of the second grade boys and even ventured into the third grade ranks a time or two. It is amazing what a little experience in fighting could do for a person, even at six years of age.

One day after witnessing one of my rumbles during recess, one of the high school boys said, "He's a tough little son of a bitch, ain't he?" Having overheard this compliment did nothing to make me behave like less of a little brat. After hearing that, I usually made a point to pick my fights when I knew that some of my high school admirers were close by. (If you want to make a show-off really rotten, put him around a bunch of high school boys!)

The scrappier boys I fought with my fists, and the ones I was sure I could whip without any trouble I only wrestled to the ground to show them that I was stronger than them. Most of the boys I whipped ended up becoming my friends afterwards. I made friends quickly with the boys I figured could whip me because I wasn't a complete dummy.

I always tried to be aware of the location of the teachers assigned to oversee the playground activities during recess periods, and made sure my fighting was around the corner of the nearest building. I knew that, if I got caught, I would get a whipping from either my teacher or the principal, so I was very cautious.

Once, I organized a team consisting of myself and two others to whip James Johnson, a third grader who had been mistreating one of my first grade friends, Charles Ray Grayson. With Charles Ray and Gene Shadic, I planned a little surprise for James, laying it out during recess one afternoon after witnessing one more unmotivated attack on Charles Ray. "I got some brass knucks at home, and I'll bring 'em tomorrow! We'll gang up on old James and tear his ass up!"

The other two boys were all for it and so it was settled. The following day would be the end of James' habit of picking on Charles Ray. I had no idea what brass knucks actually looked like because my brass knucks were individual pieces of brass pipe cut into half-inch-wide rings that were much too big for my little fingers. They were just pieces of scrap salvaged from some of Floyd's work, but I had them in my back pockets when I went to school the next day. As I showed them to Charles

Ray and Gene before school, I grinned with a devilish smile, and we planned our attack on James Johnson for the morning recess.

James was small for his age but he was still bigger than any of the three of us. His mouth was permanently twisted into a kind of tough man smirk. With a cowlick curling one side of his hair in the front and another causing the hair to stand up at the back of his head, he looked as if he were just naturally tough. As I persuaded James to come with me to the far side of the Home Economics cottage "to talk," I was nervous. James was a bit leery but he was scared of nothing and no one.

As we turned the corner at the rear of the cottage, I eased my hands into my rear pants pockets, furtively working my fingers into the brass rings, three on my right hand and two on my left. As I did so, I could imagine the effect it would have on James' face when I hit him.

Gene was the spokesman for the group because he was older than me and Charles Ray, and just about as tough as any kid around. I felt as if I had really done some good recruiting to get Gene to help me against James.

The teacher on duty, Mrs. Jones, found us there, having become suspicious when she saw four of the meanest kids in the lower grades disappearing together behind the Home Economics cottage. She had followed and hid behind some shrubbery at the corner of the building. It didn't take her long to hear enough to convince her that she was on the verge of having some serious trouble on her hands.

When she found us, we were cursing like sailors and in a standoff, with me as nervous as I could be and just dying to pop old James upside his head with those brass knucks. But, I had managed to get them off my fingers with amazing speed and into the right rear pocket of my jeans without the teacher being any wiser. Off to the principal's office we went, Mrs. Jones in the lead and herding us four little devils along in front of her like goats.

Mr. Hollis assumed his most principal-like expression after listening to Mrs. Jones' story, and then he thanked her and excused her. "I'll take care of these boys right now and I don't think you'll have any more trouble with them any time soon!"

The principal's statement made me sweat just a little bit. I was so nervous, I completely forgot about the brass knucks in my back pocket, but I didn't forget them for long. After scolding all of us severely, Mr. Hollis took me by the hand first and led me over to his chair. Then he sat down and told me to bend over his knees. With the first swing of the paddle, there was a loud clunk that surprised all present. I felt my face flush with embarrassment for two reasons—first, for my stupidity in deciding to put the knucks in my back pocket rather than my front, and secondly, for the fact that Mr. Hollis, while feeling around on my butt with his free hand, easily found the telltale lumps on the pocket.

"Boy, what's that you got in your pocket?" he asked.

"Brass knucks," I replied, trying to hide my fright and convey my innocence, while retaining a wee hint of smugness for the benefit of my partners.

After looking over the pipe scraps, and getting a bit of my meaning when I called them brass knucks, Mr. Hollis told me, "Boy, you take them home and don't you ever bring them back up here! You hear me?"

"Yes, sir!" I replied, although I hardly heard my own answer. I was too busy thinking to myself that I had just learned my first real lesson in school: never bring weapons (or so-called weapons) to school.

I was smart, but I was kind of a slow learner when it came to my schoolwork. So I wasn't Mrs. Green's favorite pupil, but we got along fine for a while. I was like a little mouse around her, barely speaking loud enough for her to hear me. I was the same way around girls. If one of them tried to talk to me, I would blush and talk as little as possible. For a little schoolyard terror and bully, I was so timid around grownups and girls, it was pathetic.

One day in the school cafeteria just a few weeks into the term, the relationship between Mrs. Green and me abruptly took a turn for the worse. The first and second graders' plates were filled and placed on the tables for us, and the food was plentiful and good and I enjoyed most of it. However, on this particular day, there was a portion of macaroni and cheese on my plate. It was the first I'd ever seen of the gooey looking substance and it looked awful to me—sort of sickening.

Mrs. Green noticed that I wasn't eating any of it and walked over to my table. "Now, Freddy Ray, you need to eat that macaroni and cheese because it's good for you!" she said, her arms folded across her chest.

"I don't want any," I replied meekly, looking down at my lap to avoid her stare. My face felt awfully warm so I knew it must have been turning red.

"Now, young man," she continued, shaking her finger at me and pointing at my plate, "I told you to eat that because it's good for you and that's what I mean for you to do!"

I didn't look up or make any attempt to eat anything at all. I just continued looking down at my lap.

Mrs. Green was enraged by my disobedience. She grabbed me by my arm, jerked me roughly from my chair, and began to violently shake me. Then she slapped me sharply across the side of my face, her fingers landing squarely on my left ear. The side of my face burned and my ear was ringing from the force of the blow, but she wasn't done with me yet. She began shaking her finger in my face again while gripping my right arm so hard with her left hand, it made me wince from the pain.

"Now, you're gonna eat that, Freddy Ray Franklin, if it's the last thing you do!" she stormed. She plopped me down forcefully into my chair and once again pointed at the macaroni and cheese. "Now eat that!"

I was hurting and scared, but I knew I could take a lot more abuse than she had dished out so far. I also knew for certain that I was not going to eat any macaroni and cheese.

While I had been on my feet taking my punishment, I had seen the looks on the faces of the high school students who were in line to get their lunches. Every single one of them seemed to be sympathetic, including my brother, Gerald. He was sitting at the table next to mine, and had a concerned look on his face that seemed to say, "Don't give up!"

I figured, *I've already been punished so I don't have to eat it,* and I became sullen once again, my hands clenched together in my lap and my chin ducked down against my chest.

Mrs. Green shook her head in dismay and turned away, realizing that my stubborn streak was too deep to combat. As she walked away, still shaking her head in disbelief, the high school students filing by whispered words of encouragement and sympathy to me, and made critical remarks about Mrs. Green. They made me feel better and I began to realize that this victory was possibly more important than any of the fights I had won previously on the schoolyard. Still, though, my face continued to burn and my ear was hurting!

This incident would remain crystal clear in my mind for a long, long time, but it was the events of the next few weeks at home that probably had more to do with that than what actually happened at school. Floyd had never seemed to take any interest in the schooling of any of us kids, but on almost a nightly basis for the next three weeks, I gave him reason to take notice—and that reason had to do with the ear boxing I had gotten at school.

Every night when I lay down in bed to sleep, my ear would start hurting and I would start to cry. My ear didn't bother me much at all during the day, but the minute I lay down at night, it would start hurting. Edra would go to the kitchen for a spoon and a bottle of olive oil, pour a small amount of the oil into the spoon, and then pour it into my ear. This would ease the pain. After the first few nights, she left the olive oil and a spoon on a nearby shelf, knowing that more than likely, she would need the olive oil on a nightly basis for a while. Otherwise, no one in the house would get any sleep.

Floyd surprised me because, rather than fussing at me for whining and crying, he carried on about what a stupid thing Mrs. Green had done, and how he would go up there and personally slap her if she ever slapped another young'un of his. He even threatened to go any-way and slap her hard enough to show her how it would feel to have an earache every night!

I knew this wouldn't have been a solution, because the problem really came about because of my stubborn-ness. But after what had transpired during the summer, I was looking for a sign of some decency and caring in my father. I was at an age where I admired my father and longed to be able to speak of him with as much respect as the other boys my age did when they talked about their fathers.

In the years to come, I would search back through my memory, trying to recall the times when Floyd had taken a vocal interest in my welfare. This would be the one incident I would have to cling to, as I wouldn't be able to come up with any others. It stood by itself.

Eight

October, 1951

In early October, the trees were beginning to paint their seasonal picture along the timberline that surrounded the Franklin farm—a scene of mixed colors forming a masterpiece that would fade away with the advent of winter, like so many of the creatures that found shelter there.

One creature that did come into prominence during this time was the squirrel. There were small, nimble cat squirrels and the bigger fox squirrels, and both were wild and plentiful in our area, providing a major source of meat for many families like ours during the winter months.

The opening day of squirrel season sounded like war in the woods, as just about every man and boy old enough to hunt was out on opening day.

Floyd was no exception—and this year was to be the first time I was asked to go along. There was sport to the hunt, but there was also a seriousness to it, for it provided the family with meat during years when there was little to eat except for the vegetables raised on the farm. I was very excited in anticipation of my first hunt.

Floyd awakened me before dawn and herded me into the kitchen for a quick breakfast before we headed across the pasture for the woods beyond the fences. I stayed right on Floyd's heels because it was so dark, I could hardly see, and I stumbled frequently, grunting each time as I fought to regain my balance to keep from falling on my face. Only once did I fall completely to the ground, but I was up before Floyd saw me. I made sure of that.

Our eyes soon became accustomed to the darkness that just preceded the dawn and I found time to gaze out through the treetops as I walked along behind Floyd. Everything seemed so peaceful. The night creatures had retreated to their hiding places and those that came out during the day (most humans included), were not yet stirring. I shivered a bit from the chill in the air but I was exhilarated by it all.

In my mind, there had been a kind of bond established between Floyd and me when he supported me when I had trouble with my teacher. Floyd kept it going that day, teaching me how to walk through the woods quietly, avoiding the twigs and dry leaves to keep the noise down to a minimum. Floyd told me, "Learning how to be real quiet when movin' through the woods is the key to bein' a good hunter." He also taught me that noise could be helpful, too.

When the first squirrel we saw spotted us, it moved around to the other side of the tree, and as long as Floyd and I stayed together, the squirrel stayed on the opposite side of the tree. "Go around yonder to the other side of the tree and make some noise," Floyd instructed. "Shake a bush or pick up a stick and throw it a little ways."

I saw the squirrel as soon as I got far enough out beyond the tree to where I could see all the way to the top of it. I grabbed a bush and began shaking it vigorously. I didn't really understand why Floyd had told me to do this until I saw the squirrel move around to the other side of the tree to hide from whatever was making the noise. Floyd easily downed the squirrel with a quick shot from his shotgun.

We continued to move quietly through the woods and repeated this several times, killing three cat squirrels and one red fox squirrel before turning back toward the farm.

I went hunting with Floyd only one or two times after that day, but I learned a lot on those few occasions and enjoyed them immensely. Floyd always had me carry the squirrel sack—the canvas bag with a shoulder strap which Edra had made from an old tarpaulin, expressly for the purpose of carrying the squirrels from the hunt.

It was after the second of these Saturday morning hunts that Floyd decided to go to the grocery store at Haile, and asked me to go along. The trip was unnecessary, but Floyd always preferred to be on the move instead of sitting at home. I jumped at the chance to go. I shared my father's urge to roam and I also looked forward to the soft drink and candy Floyd would give me as a treat on those rare occasions when he allowed me to tag along.

(I would one day know in my own mind that, had I lived during the time that Floyd was a young man, I would have probably spent some time as a hobo, just as my father had before he came to Louisiana. As it was, the urge to roam caused me to walk the five miles to Haile on Saturday afternoons beginning when I was fourteen years old. I would spend time with older boys, drinking beer and smoking, knowing all the while that most of the time, I would have to walk that five miles back home at midnight, in the dark. If I were lucky, there might be enough moonlight for me to see where I was going. Sometimes, one of the older boys who had a car would drive me home. My mother worried about me but she had no control over me, and Floyd didn't care. So, I was more or less on my own.)

The five-mile drive to Haile was uneventful, hardly a prelude to what was to follow. I was silent during the ride that took us across the same railroad tracks five times before reaching the main highway at Haile, six times if you counted the spur at the last crossing. I wondered why the road and the railroad couldn't just run along together, side by side. Then we wouldn't have had to always be afraid of getting hit by a freight train while crossing the tracks so many times.

Seeing the railroad tracks called to mind the photo of Uncle Eugene's beautiful daughter, which sat on the mantel at his house. When she was only nineteen, she was riding in a car with her boyfriend when it stalled out at a railroad crossing and was struck by a train. There had been another young couple in the car, but Uncle Eugene's daughter was the only one to suffer serious injuries. She died five days after the wreck. Although many years had passed since her death, Uncle Eugene and Aunt Wilma still mourned, and her name was mentioned by them almost every time they visited with the family.

Floyd turned right onto the main highway and drove to the last of the three stores lined up on the left side of the highway. He pulled in and parked near the water tower beside the store. I leaned forward and looked up through the windshield of the truck at the tower and said softly, as if I were talking to myself, "I wish I could climb that tower. I bet I could really see a long way from up there."

Floyd acted as though he hadn't heard me. "Come on, boy," he shouted back toward the truck as he headed inside the Brown brothers' store, which also served as the post office and community barber shop. Ferris Brown, the postmaster, would often bring out his sheet and barber tools and give a fifty-cent haircut to any man who didn't want to make that long, eight-mile trip to the real barber shop in the town of Marion.

In addition to helping to run the grocery store, Ferris' brother, Jim Ollie, worked his post as the justice of the peace. Jim Ollie had been appointed to the post to fill their father's seat upon his death during the twenties, and he had been elected and re-elected from that time forward.

There was always some good strong coffee and conversation around the wood burning heater in the center of the store. It seemed that every man around the heater that morning had a cigar, a roll-your-own Bull Durham or Prince Albert cigarette, or a dip of Garrett snuff in his mouth.

I watched a man standing by the heater shaking tobacco onto a cigarette paper from the can, which he stuck into the bib of his overalls before rolling the cigarette. I surmised that there were a lot more uses for a Prince Albert can than there were for a Bull Durham sack, and thought to myself, *I think I'll smoke Prince Albert tobacco when I get big. I don't like the smell of cigars, and that snuff dippin' seems so nasty!* Edra dipped snuff, but that didn't make it any more appealing to me.

Ferris had shouted greetings to Floyd as we entered the store, shaking his hand and patting him on the back. Then he reached down and patted me on top of my head.

"Now, which one of your boys is this one, Floyd?" he asked. "You got so many of 'em."

"This one here is Freddy Ray," Floyd replied, patting me on the head, himself. "He's my podnuh."

"Well now, Floyd, he don't look like none of your other boys. He must be the black sheep in the family," Ferris joked, chuckling.

"Well, he's more like a billy goat! He's so damned hard headed!" Floyd said, and they both laughed, as did the men around the heater. One of the men by the heater reached underneath it for a stick of firewood and added it to the fire while another took the coffee pot and emptied the grounds into a barrel nearby. "Hold on, Floyd," he said. "I'll make a fresh pot of coffee."

Floyd simply nodded and eased into the opening they had created for him at the heater. After the greetings were over, the conversation at the heater turned to boxing. They were comparing the talents of Jersey Joe Walcott and Ezzard Charles. This held my interest, but soon the conversation turned to politics and the Korean Conflict, neither of which interested me at all.

As I ambled outside the store, still entertaining thoughts of climbing the water tower, I thought, *Floyd will probably be in there for a while. And, with no one watching me, I could climb the tower and be back on the ground without anyone ever knowing.*

The tower was not very tall, with a small water tank sitting on top, supplying the store and Ferris's house adjacent to the store. I squinted up at the tank, shading my eyes from the sun, which, from my viewpoint, seemed to sit atop the tower alongside the tank. I walked over to the ladder and carefully climbed up it until I reached the platform upon which the tank rested. Then I stood up slowly, being very cautious so I wouldn't lose my balance and go over the edge.

A cool breeze blew directly against my back, causing my tousled hair to whip around and partially cover my eyes. I brushed the hair back and checked out the scenery around the village, making a complete circle around the tank, being careful not to step on any of the beer cans that had been tossed up there by the local beer drinkers on Saturday night.

I had been on the platform for only a few minutes when I heard voices from below. When I looked over the side, I saw Floyd and a man named Jack come from under the storefront and walk between the tower and the side of the store. Jack reached in behind a pile of soft drink cases stacked beside the store and pulled out a pint of whiskey, "Here, have a shot," he said, as he handed the bottle to Floyd.

"I just believe I will," Floyd said, grinning in antici-pation as he uncapped the bottle and proceeded to take a healthy swig. "Ahh! That's good stuff! That really hit the spot," he said, drooling.

"You want to ride over to Swayback?" Jack asked as he reached out for the bottle. He was a young, robust man, with a red face that I thought looked friendly.

"Hell, yeah!" Floyd replied. "That pint ain't hardly enough to whet your appetite. Let's go."

"Okay, but what you gonna do with that boy?" asked Jack, raising the bottle to take a drink.

"Hell, he can go along for the ride and stay in the truck," Floyd answered.

I had begun to ease around the water tank in order to get to the ladder when my foot bumped into a beer can on the rim of the platform, sending it tumbling off the edge. Floyd and Jack heard the noise and looked up to see what was causing it, and as they did, the can struck Floyd directly on his nose.

As he tried to avoid getting hit in that split second, Floyd lost his balance and bumped into Jack, causing them both to fall over the pile of soft drink cases stacked against the store. This caused a loud banging and screeching as the drink cases hit the tin wall and scraped it. The whiskey bottle in Jack's hand slammed into an old tire rim leaning against the wall and broke as he went down, with Floyd coming down on top of him and the drink cases. There was a loud grunt from one of them fol-lowed by several seconds of silence. Then, as Floyd began getting to his feet, he began cursing me.

"Boy, I ought to whup your butt!" he shouted up to me, as I was slowly easing over the side of the platform onto the ladder. "Look at the damned mess you done made!"

Jack had a slightly amused expression on his face intermingled with his obvious disappointment over the spilled whiskey.

As soon as my feet touched the ground, Floyd grabbed me by the shoulders and shook me as he scolded me. "What the hell do you mean, climbin' that tower, anyway? You know goddamned well you ain't supposed to be up there!"

"Come on, Floyd. He didn't mean to do that. Let's go on to Swayback." Jack was ready to get it over with and head for someplace to get more whiskey.

This got Floyd's attention, and he rather hesitantly said okay. Before he let go of me, he gave me a look I felt was going to burn a hole through me at any second, and said, "You get your ass in Jack's truck and see if you can't stay out'a trouble. You hear me?"

I was grateful to Jack for interceding on my behalf, and went directly to the truck without saying a word.

After restacking the drink cases neatly against the store, Floyd and Jack got into the pickup with me and pulled out from the store, heading south on the highway. They talked very little for the first few miles, but after they crossed the railroad tracks at Spencer, they loosened up some and even laughed about breaking Jack's bottle of whiskey.

"Floyd, for a minute there, I thought you was goin' to lick that whiskey up off the ground, glass and all," Jack said, laughing so hard that his face got even redder than normal.

"Hell, I started to, but I was afraid I would bump heads with you! By the time I saw you wudn't gonna lick it up, all the damned stuff had soaked into the ground," Floyd said, and they both had another good laugh.

I looked around at Jack with a slight grin on my face, but turned my head quickly when Jack glanced back at me. I looked straight ahead at the highway and wondered if Jack might really be mad at me over the spilled whiskey.

After a thirty minute drive to the middle of nowhere, it seemed, we reached the joint called Swayback. One look at the poor construction of the roof of the old building, and the way it swayed from age, and it was easy to understand how the place got its name. The joint was in the backwoods all by itself, but considering how much fighting and hell raising went on there, most of the local residents thought it wasn't far enough out in the woods.

When we stopped in front of the joint, Floyd pointed toward the back side of the building and said, "Boy, why don't you go 'round yonder and play in the shade of them trees?"

I climbed down from the truck and ran around back, expecting to find nothing, but I was in for quite a surprise. There by a small red oak tree was a palomino saddle horse, his bridle reins tied together around the tree. The leather of the saddle shined from lots of regular use and the brass trim looked as if it had been polished.

I eased up beside the horse and patted him on his neck, then ran my fingers through his blonde mane. It was just about the prettiest horse I had ever seen and I wished I could ride him, although such a thing seemed doubtful.

The sounds of "The Golden Rocket" by Hank Snow drifted from the joint and caught my attention, and I tried to understand the words. I liked music and listened to Floyd's radio at home as often as I could. I quit listening for the words because there was so much noise from the loud talking and laughing of the men inside, the music was almost drowned out. I sang along with Hank and when I didn't know the words, I hummed.

The music had turned my attention from the horse to the back side of the joint and as I walked toward the rear door, I noticed a man lying in the grass by the far corner of the building. He was a big man with a cowboy hat covering his face and his sharp-toed boots pointed skyward. As I walked closer to investigate, a big, gray Catahoula Cur came around the corner of the building and stopped, snarling at me. The dog's teeth were bared and he looked extremely vicious. The hair along the ridge of the dog's back stood up and he continued growling. I wanted to run but I was too scared to move.

I was much relieved to see the man reach up to remove the hat covering his face and speak to the dog. "Down, big boy," he said as he looked around and saw me standing there. "Why, he ain't big enough to be a good mouthful for you."

The man grinned as he raised himself up on one elbow and looked at me. "Boy, what are you doin' out here? Why ain't you in there drinkin' beer instead of messin' 'round out back?"

I just stood there grinning, too timid to speak.

"Now, don't try to tell me you don't drink," he said with a sly grin on his face. He stood up, stretched and brushed the grass from his clothes. "Did you think old Strike was gonna eat you up?" he asked as he noticed that I was still eyeing the dog. "Why, he won't hurt nobody. He was just protectin' me while I was sleepin' off my mornin' drunk."

I still had not said a word. I was surveying the man, noticing the nice clothes he wore—cowboy-cut khakis, a fancy plaid cowboy shirt and a laced leather belt with a big shiny buckle. I knew the man's boots were expensive because I had heard my older brothers talk about a pair of boots costing a month's wages for most men.

My grin widened once I'd been assured that the man's dog wouldn't bite.

"Who's your daddy?" the man asked.

"Floyd Franklin," I answered, staring down at the ground and shifting from one side to the other in my tracks.

"You mean Shorty Franklin? Works for Columbian Carbon, don't he?" he asked.

"Yessir," I said, still not looking up at the man. "I guess so." (He had been dubbed "Shorty" on account of his slim, five-feet-seven-inch build.)

"Yeah, I know him," he said as he started toward the rear door of the joint. "Now Strike, don't you be botherin' that boy, you hear?" The dog wagged his tail and walked a few steps toward me as if he understood perfectly what his owner was saying and was ready to make friends with me.

When the man disappeared through the back door of the beer joint, I decided I was too close to Strike, so I backed away and climbed the steps of the small porch on the back of the building. I felt a whole lot safer there and I could hear the music better, too.

The big man had pushed only halfheartedly on the door after entering the joint, leaving the door open a couple of inches and allowing me to see inside once I got up on the porch. I watched the men lined up along the bar sipping their beer and whiskey, and it seemed like most of them were trying to carry on about nine different conversations at once. I could see the jukebox over in the corner and it was about the shiniest thing I had ever seen, with all that chrome on it.

I pressed my face closer to the door and could see a table where a game was in progress. It was my first time seeing a pool table, so I didn't know exactly what I was looking at, but the two men there seemed to be having a good time playing the game.

After a while, I saw Floyd walk out the door of the bar, so I jumped off the back porch and ran around to the front of the building. I sure didn't want to be left behind. I ran to the side of Jack's pickup, stopped and turned back toward Floyd, who was nearing the truck himself.

"Hey, boy, what are you runnin' from?" Floyd asked when I looked up at him. "Is somebody after you?"

I didn't want Floyd to know that the dog, Strike, had scared me. "I just saw you leavin' and I didn't want to get left behind," I said, avoiding Floyd's eyes.

"Get in the truck," he growled, opening the truck door and pointing to the seat.

I climbed into the truck and Floyd followed, rolling down his window and slamming the door three times before it latched tightly.

Floyd stared at the front door of the joint and I stared at the floorboards of the truck for a few minutes in total silence before Jack appeared in the doorway with a fifth of whiskey in each hand. He walked over to the truck and after opening the door on the driver's side, he handed one of the bottles of whiskey to Floyd.

"Here's your jug you left in there," he muttered.

Floyd merely took the bottle of Old Crow and cradled it between his legs without speaking as Jack turned the ignition switch, and pressed the starter pedal in the floorboard with his foot, the engine grinding slowly for a few seconds before it cranked. Jack shifted into first gear and pulled onto the highway leading away from Swayback.

There was only a little chit-chat between the two men on the ride back to Haile and that was toward the end of the trip. They both took drinks from their bottles every few minutes and their tongues were beginning to loosen up by then. I wondered if something had transpired between the two men while they were at Swayback to make them angry with each other. Or, maybe my causing the loss of Jack's whiskey bottle was reason enough. I knew by now that men got awfully protective over their liquor.

When we arrived in Haile, we stopped at Jordan's Grocery, the first of three stores in the little village. It was the middle of the afternoon and Mr. Jordan, the storekeeper, was a little bit tipsy himself. On most Saturdays, he would have a bottle stashed in the feed room in the back of the store and would go back there for an occasional nip.

Floyd, Jack and Mr. Jordan crowded around the heater in the back of the store and talked while I slowly walked around the store gazing at the merchandise, winding up at the candy rack, where I stood for several minutes, staring, trying to decide which of the candy bars would be the best. Mr. Jordan noticed me and yelled across the room, "Help yourself to a bar of candy, on me!"

I immediately decided the Butterfinger would be my choice, and as I thanked Mr. Jordan and began to tear at the end of the wrapper, Floyd walked over to the drink box and slid the cover to one side. All the ice in the box had melted except for a piece about the size of a softball. I stood on my tiptoes and watched the ice bobbing up and down in the water as Floyd groped around until he found a Coke and pulled out the dripping bottle. He let it drip for a few seconds before reaching for the opener hanging by a string on the counter nearby and flipping off the top, leaving it lying on the floor where it fell. He handed the Coke to me and instructed Mr. Jordan to put it on his ticket.

Mr. Jordan went behind the counter and reached into a file box, searching through the ticket books until he found the one with "F. Franklin" scribbled across the top. He took it out and wrote down the drink, tearing the carbon copy out and handing it to Floyd, who wadded it up and threw it into the cardboard box that sat by the end of the counter, serving as a waste basket.

Jack walked over to the storekeeper while he was still behind the counter putting Floyd's ticket book back in the file. "Hey," he said, "give me a pa-pack of Luh-Luh-Luh-Luh…aah…aah…Luh-Luh-Luh-Luh-Luh…" Jack stuttered some anyway but the whiskey had made it a lot worse. There was just no way he could say Lucky Strike after drinking all that whiskey. He gave up on trying to articulate the name of his regular brand and asked for some "go-go-god-damned Camels!"

Mr. Jordan laughed softly as he handed Jack a package of Camels. "It didn't take you long to change brands," he said.

"Hell, there ain't no difference in 'em, anyway!" Jack said, as he turned and stomped out of the store, heading for his truck.

"That Jack Bolton is a character, ain't he?" Mr. Jordan said, laughing again, only louder this time.

Floyd laughed himself as he agreed with the storekeeper, and then motioned for me to follow him out the door. He walked to Jack's truck, opened the door on the right side and reached for his bottle of whiskey on the seat. "I'll see you Monday mornin'," he said to Jack as he closed the door.

"Okay," said Jack, who started the truck, then backed away from the store, turned toward the highway and drove straight across it, taking the gravel road toward Dean.

Floyd walked toward Brown's Grocery and our truck, and I fell in behind, recalling highlights of the day—the cowboy and his cur dog, the men drinking their liquor inside the Swayback, the first pool table I ever set eyes on, and the music coming from the shiny, chrome jukebox.

I smiled, feeling older than my years, but my smile quickly turned solemn when Floyd looked back over his shoulder at me and yelled, "Walk a little faster, slow-poke!"

Nine

Floyd Franklin was a man of many talents, some real and some imagined. The man who some people called Shorty was not afraid to try something new.

He was a welder, so he was skilled at fabricating metal objects for the natural gas company where he worked. Such objects were generally made of pipe or steel and were used in the gathering and measuring of gas for distribution. In his spare time, he built things like pipe fences, gates, swing sets, and metal picnic-table frames.

He also enjoyed making knives and reworking the worn parts of guns. He could take apart a gun and rework worn parts to bring them back to their original dimensions, or he could make a missing part after looking at the area where the part was to go and figuring out what purpose it served. Some of those parts had very intricate shapes, and a lot of thought and patience was required in order to build them so that they would work properly.

Floyd was the type of man who liked gadgets. He would see something that had been commercially manufactured and copy it. Many of these gadgets had very little practical use, and ended up in the iron junk pile beside Floyd's shop. A few of them left impressions of varying degrees on us boys. One gadget that he made and used for a while produced some unexpected and unwanted results that left a lasting impression on us younger boys.

Floyd called this gadget the worm getter, and it was his version of an apparatus described to him by someone at work. It was constructed of two, thirty-inch-long, quarter-inch-in-diameter bare welding rods with handles made from six-inch lengths cut from a broom handle. Single-conductor electrical cable was attached to the rods under the handles and these were spliced into an extension cord. The bottom ends of the rods were sharpened to a point by filing them.

Here's how this gadget worked: the rods were driven into the ground a couple of feet so they would reach the dampness of the soil beneath the ground's surface. They would be placed eight to ten feet apart, and then the cord would be plugged into an electrical outlet. The electrical current running through the damp soil between the rods would bring any earthworms there wiggling to the surface, where they could be picked up after the electrical cord was disconnected from the outlet. These earthworms were much bigger than the little red wigglers Floyd had in his worm bed and within a short time, he could get enough worms to go fishing.

One Saturday morning in the spring of 1952, a friend of Floyd's by the name of Crawford Colson was visiting with him. (Just like Floyd, Crawford had been given the nickname of Shorty.) After hearing about this easy method of gathering worms, he asked Floyd to demonstrate his worm getter. Floyd sent Ike into the house for the contraption while he and Shorty took a shot of whiskey from Shorty's bottle.

When Ike returned with the rods, Floyd unrolled the electrical cord and walked out away from the house as far as the cord would allow. Then he proceeded to work the rods into the ground, being very careful to get them the proper distance apart and deep enough. The deeper the rods were driven into the ground, the better they seemed to work. The ground was already damp from the overflow of a shower barrel nearby, the overflow coming as a result of Floyd pumping it full earlier in the day and temporarily forgetting about it, letting the pump run too long.

The shower barrel was on top of a metal tower which had once been the property of the gas company where Floyd worked. It had been abandoned and with a little patch work, Floyd had made it almost as good as new. (The tower was identical to many others in the low-lands along the river, each about eight-to-twelve-feet high, six-foot square at the base, four-foot square at the top, and made of pipe. Given the abundance of natural gas wells in the area and the propensity of the Ouachita River to flood, these towers were required to elevate the gas meters so they would not become submerged during flooding.)

After retrieving and restoring the abandoned tower, Floyd had set it up and placed a fifty-five-gallon barrel on top of it. He fabricated a shower head that was about six inches in diameter and connected this to the bottom of the barrel with a straight length of pipe. The tower stood about twelve feet tall and the pipe and shower head extended down to a point which was just over six feet from the ground.

There was a valve placed in the line just above the shower head for turning it on and off, and some scrap roofing tin installed around the bottom half of the tower, with a piece of canvas hung at the door opening on one corner. The shower stall was a little less than six feet square. To keep you from getting your feet muddy when showering, boards were placed on the ground for floor-ing.

The biggest drawback to this open-air bath house was the danger from snakes that sometimes hid in the tall grass and weeds around the edges of the stall or under the boards that served as the floor. The regular wetting of the ground around the stall made the grass grow and it also attracted frogs, which could be a real nuisance when you used the shower.

If you got into the shower and didn't have frogs hopping across your feet or snakes slithering by during the first minute or so, you could be fairly certain that you wouldn't be bothered, and could then concentrate on your shower and enjoy it. But you could never be positive of a nuisance-free shower, and at times there were showers cut short by the sight of a snake trying to escape the water flowing out the sides of the stall.

Of course, the only time this shower could be used was during periods of hot weather, because the water was simply too cold if it had not been warmed during the day by the hot sun. Even when the water temperature wasn't an issue, there could be no more than two showers taken each afternoon, because the barrel would be empty before a third person could finish their shower. Therefore, most times, us Franklin children continued to take our baths in the galvanized wash tub in the far corner of the kitchen, where hot water could be added to the tub from the kettle fetched from the stove nearby. Or, we would simply bathe with a washcloth, using water from a wash pan on the washbasin stand.

On that particular morning, Floyd had pumped the shower barrel full of water with a recently installed water pump, which was powered by pressure from the natural gas well on the farm. When it overflowed, the cascading water had wet a large area surrounding the tower, including the area where Floyd had placed the worm-getter rods—a place where the yard was mostly void of grass.

Floyd was shirtless and shoeless, and after he completed driving the rods into the ground, he backed away from the rods the distance typically considered safe, and instructed Ike to plug in the extension cord. In the same breath, he told Shorty, "Now, you just watch and see what happens!"

Floyd proceeded to put on quite a performance. As soon as the cord was plugged in, Floyd began to jump up and down and dance around as fast as he could, stuttering and stammering, trying to say something. He had backed away from the rods the normally safe distance, but he had failed to take into consideration two important facts—the ground surface was usually pretty dry when he used the worm getter, and he usually wore shoes. This time, with all the dampness around from the overflow of the shower barrel, the electrical charge traveled much further than usual through the ground.

Floyd's bare feet were taking a direct charge and he was really dancing a jig. Mike, Gerald, Terry Gene, and I stood watching and wondering what had happened to Floyd. We had never seen him acting so strange and we thought it was kind of funny—but then we saw Shorty's reaction and we knew something was wrong. Shorty was on the opposite side of the wet area from the back door of the house and was reluctant to attempt to cross the area where Floyd was dancing. He yelled out for Ike.

By now, Ike had appeared in the doorway and was watching Floyd himself, wondering what he was doing. Floyd appeared to be trying to tell Ike something, but he was making no sense at all with his gibberish.

Shorty yelled for Ike to unplug the cord and as Ike turned to go into the house, he looked back toward Floyd, really intrigued by the show he was putting on, and not realizing the seriousness of the matter. He hesitated when Floyd began pointing at him and trying to speak again.

The hesitation on Ike's part was too much for Floyd and it caused him to regain his voice. "Un-un-un-un-un-un-pl-pl-plug the son of a bitch!" he yelled at the top of his voice.

Ike reacted quickly then. He understood perfectly what Floyd wanted now, and he ran inside to unplug the extension cord. When Ike returned to the doorway, Floyd had stopped his dancing and immediately began chastising him.

"Why the hell didn't you unplug the damned thing when you saw it was shockin' me? Hell, slow as you are, it could'a killed me while you was standin' there like a damned fool!"

Ike stood in the doorway without answering and hung his head, bracing himself for a further verbal assault.

Now that everything seemed to be okay, Shorty started grinning, saying, "Hell, Floyd, I didn't know you could dance like that! Fred Astaire couldn't hold a candle to you. But I don't see no worms anywhere."

Floyd wasn't amused at all, and he pulled up the rods, rolled the cord around them and threw them onto the back porch before answering Shorty.

"It wouldn't be so damned funny if you were the one gettin' your ass shocked!" he said as he turned to Shorty. But there was a slight smile on his face as he walked by the other man and reached for the bottle of whiskey sitting in a nearby chair.

Ike turned and walked into the house, and when he did, the rest of us boys followed him. When we got inside, we went to a window and peeped out at Floyd, and then got to one side of the room away from the window and began dancing and shuddering and stammering, mocking Floyd's movements while he was being shocked. We were laughing as hard as we dared, trying to contain our laughter so that Floyd wouldn't hear us, because we knew that if he saw us mocking him, he would tear our butts up.

Later on that morning, Floyd stuck his head in the back door and yelled for us boys to come out into the yard and bring the boxing gloves. Someone he worked with had given him a couple pairs of old gloves and he delighted in seeing us spar. He wanted Shorty to see what a show we could put on.

Ike and Mike were small for their age; in fact, Gerald and I were almost as big as they were, even with the difference in our ages. There were no real mismatches between any of us, but the twins definitely had an advantage on us younger two. They always won any fights with Gerald or me, but we never let them walk away without a few aches, pains, and bruises to remind them that their little brothers might have been younger but we weren't quitters.

For the next hour, while Floyd and Shorty sipped their whiskey, we entertained them with boxing matches that left no real winners but did provide quite a show. There were a few scratches caused by the curled up corners of ripped gloves and a little blood from a nose or two, but we fought willingly and enjoyed it until we were almost totally exhausted.

One of the areas where Floyd imagined he had talent was in his ability to be a barber. When Raymond Day, who was Floyd's nephew and also a professional barber, gave him some well-used manual clippers and barber shears, he became an overnight, self-proclaimed expert in this field. It seemed only natural that Floyd would get involved in the business of cutting hair, since he had so many sons, but we dreaded the times when Floyd would bring out his hair-cutting tools. Usually, his awareness of when we boys were getting a little bit shaggy happened to coincide with times when he had been drinking, and this didn't help his untrained hands.

If the weather was warm enough to allow it, Floyd would hold his barbering sessions out in the yard under the shade of a huge pecan tree, allowing us to avoid having to sweep up after our haircuts. If there happened to be a breeze blowing, the whole affair was made a little more pleasant.

Nobody wanted to have Floyd cut their hair, and my brothers and I would usually argue about who was going to go first. But, when he got ready to go, Floyd would grab whoever was within easy reach, lead him to the straight-back, cane-bottom chair, and get the show on the road. He would take an old sheet he kept in his kit and pin it with a safety pin after cinching it around the neck so tightly that it almost choked the one about to receive a haircut.

The haircuts we had always received from Gramma or Edra left our hair long enough to comb, but after Floyd received his barber kit, long hair became a thing of the past. The process would begin with Floyd clipping onto the clippers the attachment designed to give a G.I. cut. He would go through our hair with this attachment, leaving the hair a quarter inch in length all over. That part was usually okay, but what followed could be kind of rough. The word torture seems like a legitimate description of what we went through when Floyd began trimming around the ears and the back of the neck.

Floyd would place the clippers tight against the skin down low on the neck, and up he would go, pinching and pulling and cutting hair and frequently nicking the scalp. This wasn't the worst part, though. The part that really hurt was preceded by a warning of sorts, which did nothing to lessen the pain. After clipping up the side of the head with the bare clippers, the hair would build up on the top of the clippers, blocking Floyd's view so that he could not clearly see where he was cutting. When this happened, he would first slow down his clipping motion, and then stop for a split second. This short pause was the warning for the haircut recipient to get set and clench his teeth for what was to come next.

At this point, Floyd would suddenly flip his wrist outwards with the air of a professional, and throw the hair from the clippers. When the clippers left the side of the head, they pulled out however many hairs happened to be caught between the dull blades. There could be anywhere from one to a half dozen hairs pulled out, leaving you sitting there red-faced, with your eyes bugged out from the choking you were getting from the tightness of the sheet around your neck, and in terrible pain. Just imagine several hairs being pulled from your head at once, all from the same spot! One time would have been plenty, but this usually happened several times during one of Floyd's haircuts.

At the end of this torture, relief came in stages. As Floyd picked up the round, long-bristled brush that had come with his kit, the brother receiving the haircut would brace himself for the thrashing that came as Floyd began briskly brushing the hair off his ears, neck and face. Somehow, before he was finished, Floyd always managed to bang us on the head a few times with the wooden base of the brush handle.

Floyd completed the brushing operation in a cloud of talcum powder, shaking such enormous amounts of the sweet-smelling stuff into the brush before dusting us with it that sometimes we thought we might choke to death on the dust. At least the powder stopped or slowed the bleeding from the nicks and scratches that had been inflicted upon us.

The dust wouldn't have cleared before Floyd would unpin the sheet, and as the one just finished stood up with the blood rushing to his head after removal of the death hold the sheet had on his throat, Floyd would pop the sheet in the breeze with a flourish. As this action caused us to be showered with the hair flying from the sheet, Floyd would look around and yell, "Next!"

I hated these haircuts worse than anybody, and I would usually give the next brother after me a look that seemed to say, "Now it's your turn. Suffer, because I had to!" I could never seem to help being just a little bit mean.

Even worse than the haircut was the feeling I got when I looked in the mirror at my scratched, nearly hairless, gapped-up head and thought of the embarrassment I would suffer at school until my hair grew out sufficiently enough to hide the gaps in the uneven cut. This probably accounted for the fact that, as I grew older, I had longer hair than most boys.

I continued to be troubled by the things I saw around me in everyday life and by the things I heard from my older brothers concerning Floyd and his volatile disposition. I looked for the good in my dad and was puzzled by the meanness that sometimes erupted in him. My brothers and I were all afraid of Floyd, but at times he would surprise us with acts of kindness.

One such act occurred during the winter prior to the spring of 1952 when Floyd bought a pair of baby goats and presented them to Gerald and me. My brother picked the little billy, a beautiful white animal with lots of black blanketing his back, and mine was the little female that was mostly white.

Floyd made a small house from scrap lumber for the goats to sleep in and bought hay so Gerald and I could make beds for them in their little house. It was the first time we had pets to call our very own, and we were very happy little boys. During the week, our school days always ended with the thought of getting home so we could check on our goats and play with them until suppertime.

I would always remember this as one of the happiest times in my childhood, despite the fact that it brought with it another life lesson I probably could have learned in a much easier manner.

It began at a time when there were fresh, springtime leaves and buds on all the trees and bushes around the farm, but hardly anything growing inside the pasture thanks to the mule, the old black milk cow, and at times, hogs that passed through on their way to the family table. The goats, tiring of the meager pickings within their confines, found their way out of the pasture and took to the woods, feeding on those young leaves and buds.

Our goats had disappeared during the day in the middle of the first week of April, and when we got home from school that day and found them gone, we were devastated. We began to imagine all sorts of bad things that could happen to goats out there somewhere in the woods at night. We were afraid a panther might get them, despite assurances from Gramma that no panther had been spotted in the area for at least the past thirty years.

We searched the woods around the pasture as far as we dared in the short time we had before dark, but we found nothing and received only discouraging remarks from the twins, who were a bit jealous of Gerald and me. As we came into the house that night, almost in tears, Mike told us, "Y'all won't ever see them kids again."

Gerald didn't do anything but I ran over to where Mike sat on the end of the bench alongside the dinner table and, before he knew what was happening, I hit him on the side of his head as hard as I could.

"Why, you little..." Mike growled as he recovered from the surprise attack, holding his hand over the stinging bruise on the side of his face. He made a dive for me and was just beginning to choke me when Edra grabbed him from behind and pulled him off me.

"He hit me!" Mike yelled, struggling with Edra, still trying to get at me.

"Just hold on! I won't have this fightin' in my kitchen!" Edra said. "Freddy Ray, you get out of here! You know better than that!" She held Mike until I made my way past him, shooting him a belligerent stare as I went by.

"I'll get him for this!" Mike said as he watched me disappear through the door into the room where five of us younger boys crowded together to sleep at night. But that night, Edra would be watching, and there would be no revenge—at least not yet.

By the time Saturday rolled around, the whole family was just about sick of hearing Gerald and me (mostly me) worry over our pets. Edra had talked Floyd into helping us look for our goats on Saturday morning.

We were really surprised when Floyd told us at breakfast that he was planning to help us find our goats that day. I hadn't dreamed of asking him because we always assumed that you simply did not ask for, or expect, any sympathy or favors from Floyd. Just about the time I had begun to see the reasoning behind my brothers' beliefs, Floyd did something to contradict them.

The search carried us a mile through the woods to the rear of the farm, up and down all the pipelines and the narrow roads to the individual gas wells that were located here and there, one being on almost every forty-acre tract in the area. We found tracks and evidence of the goats feeding on the lower tree limbs and bushes throughout the area, but we did not see our pets.

After walking for several hours, Floyd was tired and so were we, but he was more anxious to quit the search than Gerald or me. We knew when Floyd turned back toward the main pipeline that would lead back to the farm that it would do no good for us to ask him to search further. We ran ahead, hoping that our goats had worked their way back toward home.

When we were within half a mile of home, I ran out into the woods for a couple hundred feet in order to see as much of the area as I could without getting far enough out that I might get disoriented and lose my way. When I was working my way back to the pipeline further up through the woods, I came to a spot that had little timber on it, an area about a hundred feet across. There was a lot of brush and weeds there and it was so thick I could only see a few yards ahead of myself. I went through the middle of it and to my surprise, I did not find any sign of our goats having been there. It looked as if it would have been such an ideal spot for them to get all they wanted to eat, and it was so close to home!

I felt as if I really would never see my pet again. As I came out of the dense growth and neared the tall timber, I found some bushes growing together in an area about the size of our hog pen in back of the barn. The bushes had no limbs on them and they were twice as tall as me. They had leaves growing all along their long slender stems, but not a single limb, unless you called the three or four twigs at the very top of them limbs. I leaned over and broke off the tallest of them along the edge of the growth. I began to strip it of its leaves as I continued on my path toward the pipeline and home.

By the time I got back to the pipeline, I had stripped all the leaves off the long switch except for those on the twigs at the very tip of it. I was swinging it like a whip and popping it at the deer flies as they flew by. When I looked up and down the pipeline, I saw Gerald behind me and beyond him, I could see Floyd sitting on a stump, resting.

I walked slowly toward home until Gerald caught up with me and then I picked up my pace to match his. I was disappointed that we had not found our goats and I was also feeling mischievous, since I had more energy to burn and Gerald seemed to be almost as tired as Floyd. When we had gone beyond a slight curve in the pipeline, I could see that we were out of Floyd's line of sight.

It had been several minutes since a deer fly or a bumble bee had flown close enough to swat at and I was wanting to pop something with my switch whip, so I turned and popped at Gerald's knees with it, barely touching him.

"Quit!" Gerald said, jumping backwards a couple of feet to get away from the switch. He glared menacingly, trying to bluff me.

I laughed at his reaction and ran toward him and popped at his legs again, stinging him this time.

He was too tired to put up with my foolishness and he knew it was useless to try to fight me so he ran back toward the curve, hoping maybe the sight of Floyd would deter me. That did the trick, for when I saw what Gerald was doing, I turned and sprinted toward home.

I was not to be outdone, so I planned a surprise for Gerald when he got to the house. I went through the small screened-in back porch and stepped into the kitchen. There was no one in the room, so I stood just inside the door where I could peep around through the ragged, sagging screen wire on the porch and watch Gerald approaching. As my brother entered the yard through a gate that looked as if, at any time, it might fall off the post to which it was attached, I saw that Floyd had not yet come out of the woods.

When Gerald stepped up on the porch and the screen door slammed behind him, I sprang from my hiding place inside the kitchen and began popping at him with my switch. Gerald was caught off guard and jumped to one side, winding up on the corner of the porch with me and my switch between him and any route of escape.

I was laughing a devilish laugh as I popped the switch at Gerald's legs and he fought to grab it with his hands. I would fake as if I were going to pop him in the face with the switch, and then I would quickly whip the end of it toward the tops of his bare feet, bringing little red splotches where the switch struck them.

Gerald was saying nothing. He was concentrating on the swinging, lashing switch, trying to catch it as I swung it at him, but he was getting frustrated. He was tired and totally exasperated, and I continued to laugh.

Neither of us saw Floyd approaching until it was too late for me. I was drawing back my arm for another whipping motion when Floyd grabbed my arm from behind and wrestled the switch away from me. Things were not at all funny to me anymore.

Floyd turned me around, got me by my left arm, and motioned for Gerald to get out of the way. My brother quickly exited the porch, stepping into the kitchen, where he stopped and watched what happened until he could stand no more of it. For what he witnessed wasn't pleasant, despite the knowledge that I had it coming on account of what I had been doing to him.

Floyd whipped me with my own switch just as hard and as fast as he could. The end broke off but this only made the switch easier to switch back and forth. I was squirming and crying and trying to pull loose from Floyd's grip, but he held on and beat me with the switch until I quit crying and gritted my teeth, my breathing becoming gasps for air through my clenched teeth.

When Floyd saw that he had hurt me about all he could, he quit switching me and roughly shoved me through the door of the screened-in porch and out into the yard, where I fell down in the dust bed caused by the chickens and their daily scratching around the doorsteps.

I surely had a little of the devil in me; otherwise I would not have been as mean as I was to Gerald. And I proved it when I stood up, still gritting my teeth, and dusted off my pants. I glared up at Floyd who was standing on the porch looking down at me, breathing loudly from the exertion he had put forth in whipping me. The sight of him standing there with that satisfied grin on his face made me so mad, it momentarily erased any fear of Floyd I might normally have harbored.

I put my hands on my hips and with all the bitterness a six-year-old could muster, I looked into Floyd's eyes and said, "You goddamned old son of a bitch!"

Floyd jumped as soon as I spoke, and started down the steps, saying, "I'll show you who's an old son of a bitch!"

Realizing the serious mistake I had just made, I broke into a dead run around the back side of the house. Looking over my shoulder, I could see Floyd running after me, but I was quick on my feet and he was tired after the distance covered that morning. I watched my lead steadily increasing over Floyd as I completed my second circle around the house. I had never seen Floyd run before. I was surprised by the sight of my father running after me, and one look at the vicious, determined expression on his face reminded me that I had just made a serious error in judgment.

Floyd was still there, running as hard as he could. But I was feeling a little bit more certain of my ability to gain ground, so I began to think more clearly, and immediately devised a plan. I could turn on a little bit more steam and get far enough ahead of Floyd to get out the back gate, and then I could take advantage of my speed and complete my getaway across the fields.

So, this is what I did as I looked over my shoulder one last time to check Floyd's position. If someone had put a stopwatch on me then, I surely would have broken some sprinting speed records. I encountered only one slight hitch on my last trip around the house when our family's big Rhode Island Red Rooster fluttered out from behind the chimney as I ran by. I was quick enough to make the adjustment mid-stride and clear the rooster with a short leap, but I nearly tripped and fell afterwards. It was hard to tell which one of us was more frightened by the near collision, the rooster or me, but I quickly recovered and resumed my escape, full speed.

I was really flying by the time I rounded the last corner of the house and headed directly for the gate leading from the yard to the field on the right of the garden. I had made a tremendous increase in my lead over Floyd. When I reached the gate, I ran into what at first appeared to be only a minor problem. The gate was fastened with a chain looped over a nail in the gatepost, and it was almost out of reach over my head. As I stood there fumbling with the chain, unable to get it off the big nail which was bent in two different places, causing more difficulty in removing the chain, all my feelings of security vanished along with my lead and my chances of escaping.

My hands were still on the chain when Floyd grabbed me. Up until that moment, I thought I'd already received a pretty bad whipping, but when Floyd got through with me for the second time that day, I was hurting and I was crying, and I knew that I had really been whipped. I also knew that it wasn't very smart for a six-year-old boy to call his father a son of a bitch!

The little goats returned to the farm the following week, but our joy at their return was short-lived. Two months later, Floyd sold Gerald's goat. And on the Fourth of July, he slaughtered and barbecued the one belonging to me. That was the one and only time we ever had pets to call our own.

Ten

Late 1952/Early 1953

W ithin a few weeks, things had pretty well returned to normal at home. True to form, I had dismissed from my mind that which had happened in the past—as much as I possibly could, anyway. Each day was a new adventure for me, and most days meant a new headache for Edra, since she had to police me. She had come to cherish those times when I wasn't creating havoc or otherwise causing problems for anyone.

Sometimes I would go into Floyd's room when he was gone, turn on his radio and lie down on the bed. I would clasp my hands together behind my head and stare up at the ceiling, listening to country music for hours on end. Edra would look in on me occasionally, just peeking around the door frame, feeling that sense of peace that came from knowing that I was there, and that, if I was lying on the bed listening to music, everything else around the farm was probably okay for the time being.

When I emerged from that room, it usually meant trouble for somebody because all that laying around would leave me rested and full of pent-up energy that had to be spent. I might get an empty coffee jug, place it in some corner of the yard, and throw rocks at it from a distance until it broke into pieces, leaving the glass scattered where sooner or later it would cut the bare feet of one of my brothers. (In those days, coffee was sold in glass jugs, which were about eight inches wide, ten inches high, and rounded at the corners with a wide-mouth opening.)

Wouldn't you know it, once while running from Edra, who had a switch after me, I ran through one such broken jug, cutting my feet so badly that Edra almost fainted at the sight of so much blood. Fortunately, my brother, John R., was home on leave from the Air Force and was there at the time with transportation, for I had to be taken to the doctor at Marion for stitches.

At other times, I might harass Ike and Mike or Gerald or Terry Gene—anything to get a reaction so I would have to fight or run. It seemed like I had to do something to burn up all that energy, and most times, Edra eventually had to get involved in one way or another.

Time drifted by slowly and spring turned into summer. As the heat and humidity both continued to rise and sap the energy from everyone and everything, time slowed its pace even more. On weekends when Floyd was welding or working around his shop, I was usually close by, ready to run and fetch anything that he needed, but even that came to a near standstill by July. To me, it seemed as though nothing moved in the hot summer afternoons but the flies and the steady stream of cows' tails, horses' tails, and human hands, swatting away at them.

In August, Popeye, Gerald, Terry Gene, the twins, and I would get together in the late afternoon and play softball or baseball in the pasture, using bats made from boards or white oak saplings cut from the nearby woods. The open range hogs that roamed about freely would sometimes pass through the pasture, rooting up the ground everywhere and turning it so rough that a ground ball would make some of the craziest turns as it bounced along. My brothers and I hated it when the ground got roughened up, but not enough to motivate us to fix the holes in the fence to prevent other people's hogs from getting into the pasture.

We had patched up the holes in the fence before, when other people's hogs were getting into our pasture, and then Floyd bought some pigs himself and put *them* in the pasture. Before those pigs had gotten big enough for slaughtering, they made just as big a mess of the small pasture as the neighbors' hogs. The ground continued being uneven no matter what we did. So later on, when holes were again torn in the fence by other people's hogs, we had no incentive to patch the holes. We figured that the minute we did, Floyd would just go out and buy some hogs of his own, and our hogs would root up the pasture instead of the neighbor's hogs, continuing the process. We all decided to play ball anyway, and hoped for a line drive or a fly ball, rather than a ground ball when we were in the field.

I was glad when summer was finally over that year because I wanted to get back in school. For one thing, I wanted to play softball on even ground for a change, and I also missed the friends I had made at school. Spending three months on the farm without ever going anywhere had been awfully dull in comparison to the things I'd experienced during my first year in school.

School came and with it came some disappointment, for the second grade wasn't living up to the fun I remembered from the first grade. Nevertheless, it beat staying at home all the time, and I did enjoy it. I was almost as shy as I'd always been while away from home, but I began to loosen up some, and made more friends. As my new friends shared details of their lives with me, I tried to figure out if they were more or less fortunate than I. It seemed that those who had more to be thankful for than I outnumbered those who were less fortunate, and then there were those I simply could not figure out at all.

Rusty Hodges was one of those I could not understand. I had never seen anyone like him, and after that school year, I would never see anyone like him again.

Rusty would beg other boys to hit him in his stomach as hard as they could, just to show them that he was tough, and most of the boys would oblige. Some of the older boys would send him flying backwards, but he would get up and grin at them, saying, "See? I told you that you couldn't hurt me!"

If Rusty couldn't get anyone interested in punching him, he resorted to all sorts of weird things to prove that he was immune to pain. He would run and throw himself down on the hard clay in the school yard, where he would bounce along as far as his momentum would carry him, letting his arms and legs fly where they may, refusing to protect himself from the fall. Or, he would jump against the wall on the back of the school maintenance shop, let his body slide down the wall, and fall into the ditch created from years of rainfall running off the roof onto the clay below.

Rusty would always get up smiling, after first pretending to be hurt. Then he would laugh and dare any of the boys who happened to be watching to try the same thing. He never got any takers. I considered myself tough, but I knew that I was nowhere near as tough as Rusty. I also knew that it didn't make much difference who was the tougher one. I felt the same as the other boys—Rusty was not so much tough as he was crazy!

I did notice one thing about Rusty that puzzled me. For all of Rusty's toughness and bravado, he really was a peace-loving person who never, ever attempted to start a fight. The few times he was challenged by one of the other boys, he refused to fight. Rusty's family moved away before the school year was over, but he made an impression on me that would stay with me always.

Winter came and the cracks in the walls of the old house brought the cold right inside where you could feel it without having to go outside. Thankfully, Gramma and

Edra's years of stitching together clothing scraps to make quilts made it bearable. And winter also brought us something to look forward to—Christmas.

My sister, Elizabeth, would come home from New Orleans each year at Christmas and she would have a new pair of blue jeans for each of us boys, and a dress for Myra Lou. Elizabeth seemed sort of like a stranger to me because she had graduated from high school and left for New Orleans when I was so young, and I only saw her when she came home for Christmas each year.

There were various things I noticed about Elizabeth while she was home. For one thing, she was a serious person who seemed to always be trying to impress upon us boys the fact that there was a civilization out there we would one day have to face, and we might as well start practicing behaving in a civilized manner while we were still at home. She seemed to want something better for us. I also noticed that there was a closeness between her and Gramma and Edra but she placed a distance between herself and Floyd. I wondered about that.

Christmas would pass and life would go on as usual, with the family cooped up in the house most of the winter. My older brothers could break the monotony by hunting, but us younger ones could only stay close to the fire when not in school.

In January most of the hunting seasons ended and, with few hunters in the woods with their dogs, it was safe to put out traps without fear of catching someone's deer dog, so trapping moved from the swamps out into the bayous and creeks in the hill country. Floyd trapped the ponds and creeks between home and Haile each season and usually did pretty well for the time invested.

A good mink hide would yield anywhere from ten to eighteen dollars and a coon hide about four or five dollars. During the trapping season, Floyd would pick up a couple hundred dollars extra money from the sale of hides, but the family never really realized much difference in their lifestyle because of it.

I would watch Floyd skin out the animals and stretch the hides over frames he had whittled out of thin boards from apple crates. Floyd would instruct me in how to scrape the hides clean without cutting them after he had stretched them inside out over the frames. In a few days, the hides would be stiff and he would remove the frame for use with another hide.

Floyd checked his traps each morning on his way to work and when he came home in the evening, he would skin whatever he had caught. But on Saturday mornings, he left early to run his traps and most times he was gone for a half day or longer. He would go on to Haile and meet some of his drinking buddies, and they would either finish off the whiskey he had bought the day before or go to Swayback and get more.

On those Saturday mornings when I was invited to go along, I would jump at the chance because I loved to watch Floyd work the trap lines. If he had a good catch, Floyd would be in a good mood, and if his catch was poor, his mood usually matched, but I always learned something when I went along.

One Friday evening in early February, Floyd asked me if I wanted to go with him to run his traps the next morning. I assured him at once that I did, and went about the business of laying out extra socks and shirts for the following morning in order to be prepared for the cold.

We were up early and at the break of day we were on our way, on a cold gray morning that caused me to shiver as I stumbled down the embankment from the gravel road to the creek where the first of the traps were set. I was carrying Floyd's hunting ax that had a square hammer head opposite the cutting edge. This was the only tool he needed for trapping—the hatchet edge for cutting saplings for staking the traps, and the hammer side to drive the stakes or finish off any raccoon or mink that was caught.

Floyd warned me to stay behind him because, if you weren't careful, you could be attacked by a mad raccoon. The chains on the traps weren't much over a foot long, but a lunging raccoon could seem to stretch that distance if the stake was so small in diameter that it leaned when pulled against. And occasionally, there would be a bobcat in a trap, and they were extremely dangerous. So you had to be careful when approaching an animal in one of the traps.

"I see something in that first trap yonder," Floyd whispered as we made our way through the woods along the creek bank.

I strained my eyes as I searched along the water's edge for whatever Floyd had seen. When I spotted the trapped animal, I whispered loudly, "I see him—it's a big old rabbit!"

"Well, I believe you're right. I got to bring you with me all the time...your eyes are so good."

Floyd's praise made me feel as if I were a really big help. I watched intently as Floyd knocked the rabbit out, removed him from the trap, and said, "Here, you carry him to the truck."

He started to reset the trap, but after setting the trigger, he decided to move the trap downstream a few yards. He pulled the sapling stake from the mud and, with the ring end of the trap's chain still around it, he moved the sapling and trap to a shallow spot downstream about thirty feet, within eighteen inches of the water's edge. He eased the trap into the water, which was only about three inches deep, and stuck the sharpened end of the stake as deep into the mud as he could on the side of the trap opposite the creek bank.

Floyd looked around for a moment and spotted a two-foot piece of driftwood about four inches in diameter a few feet away. "Bring me that chunk," he said, and as I did so, he explained his reasons for wanting the driftwood.

"You see," he said as he placed one end of the limb near the trap and the other end toward the creek bank, "when a mink comes through here, he'll walk around the end of this limb—he won't step over it—and he'll step right in the trap."

Floyd gently placed a few wet leaves in the water over the trap, broke a limb from a bush nearby, erased his tracks from the creek bank, and splashed water up on this to give it a more undisturbed look. Then he walked down the creek a few yards before stepping out of the water.

"Now, I ought to have a mink in that trap tomorrow mornin' for sure," he said as we headed on down the creek.

A hundred yards downstream, there was a mink in a trap set in the rotten top of a log alongside the creek. He was still alive and frightened and began to fight against the trap as we approached. Floyd eased up and placed his left hand on the stake holding the trap, then with the hatchet, he made a quick downward motion, striking the mink's head with the flat side, rendering him lifeless. He was extra careful in doing this because he didn't want to miss his mark and cut the mink's hide. A cut along the neck or back would make the hide worth only half as much as an unscarred one.

"Boy, that's a nice one," Floyd said, holding up the mink and admiring the size and quality of the hide. "He ought to bring about eighteen dollars."

I felt kind of sorry for the animal, but I didn't dwell on it as I watched Floyd reset the trap. I knew that this was a normal part of Floyd's life.

"I probably won't catch nothin' else here for a week or two," said Floyd after completing the job. "Let's get on back to the truck. This is the last trap set here."

It's about time! I'm about to freeze to death! I thought, sticking my cold hands into my pockets, and holding the rabbit's rear feet against my side with my arm in order to carry him. As we walked toward the truck, I dropped the rabbit several times, so I finally began dragging the rabbit along, first with my right hand while my left hand stayed in the warm front pocket of my jeans, then switching hands when my right hand got too cold.

The next creek was about two miles down the road and in checking the traps there, we found raccoons in two of the six traps. By the time we got through checking and resetting those traps, a slow, cold rain had begun falling and we were almost soaking wet when we got back to the truck.

The first thing Floyd did when he got into the truck was reach under the seat, pull out a paper bag holding a fifth of Old Crow, and take a drink. He grunted with satisfaction as he replaced the cap on the bottle of whiskey and jammed it back under the seat.

As Floyd cranked the truck and headed down the road toward Haile, the truck's heater took the chill from my nose and hands. My feet still felt cold as ice, but as I gazed out the back window at the mink, rabbit, and raccoons lying in the rain in the back of the truck, I didn't feel quite so cold.

Upon arriving in Haile, Floyd pulled in beside Jordan's Grocery, exited the truck quickly, and ran through the rain into the store. I was right on his heels, both of us dripping water across the un-level floor as we headed to the heater at the far end of the grocery aisle.

After greeting us, Mr. Jordan walked over to the drink box, removed a Coca Cola and opened it, and then motioned for Floyd to go into the feed room. I knew they would come out of there smelling of whiskey. Floyd's mood had already brightened up after the drink he had taken earlier. It didn't matter to me what they did because I had other things on my mind. With Floyd's permission, I helped myself to a strawberry soda and a Butterfinger, stashing the candy to savor later.

There was no one else around the store, so Floyd and Mr. Jordan talked quietly for a few minutes by the heater while I gazed through the glass in the front door, watching the rain fall on the highway that passed within ten feet of the gas pump at the front of the store.

We soon left the store and Floyd drove across the highway, over the railroad tracks, turned the corner, and pulled over by the side of the road in front of a large old weather-beaten house with a porch across half the front. The yard showed evidence of once having been well cared for, but now the junk lying in the dried-out grass and weeds and the leafless branches of the many trees and shrubs gave the place a slightly haunted look.

"This is where Shorty Waldrop lives," Floyd informed me, as a small, wiry man appeared on the porch. I could see from his physique where he got his name—he was shorter than Floyd. He was also skinny, and it looked like his belt was the only thing keeping his pants from falling down around his feet.

To my surprise, Charles Ray Grayson came through the door behind Shorty. (I would later come to find out that Charles Ray and his mother only lived with Shorty Waldrop for less than a year. She was a woman who went from man to man and stayed on the move.) My classmate had seen Floyd before, but he didn't realize that he was my father.

"That boy and his momma live with Shorty," Floyd said as he opened the truck door. "Come on. Let's go visit a spell."

"Yeah, he's in my class at school," I said as I bounced out of the truck and ran to the gate which was open and looked as if it might fall off its hinges if you touched it.

Charles Ray smiled and came down the high steps to greet us. "Y'all come on in out of the rain," he said as he pointed to the door.

My first impressions of the house being like a haunted house were reinforced as we went through the torn, rusty screen door into a large cold room with a high ceiling. The room was completely devoid of any furniture.

Shorty directed us through a door on the left side of the room into a large kitchen decorated with a bare table and three cane-bottom chairs. At the table sat a woman I had never seen before. She was an attractive woman and when she stood up, I noticed that her dress was shorter than any dress I had ever seen and it was cut low at the top. I felt myself blush as I realized that I was staring at the roundness of the skin showing from the V-neck of the dress. I looked down at my feet until Floyd spoke.

"Mary, this here is Freddy Ray," said Floyd. "He's my main sidekick." He placed his hand under my chin and raised my face up so that Mary could see it.

"Why, hello there, Freddy Ray. I've heard a lot about you from Charles Ray," she said, smiling at me.

I smiled timidly as I ducked my head again and turned back toward Charles Ray, who stood just inside the kitchen door.

Mary reached for her coffee cup on the table and walked over to the stove, picking up the coffee pot. "How about a cup of coffee, Floyd?"

"No. I don't believe," Floyd replied, raising both hands up in front of him.

"Well, if you don't want coffee, how about a drink of whiskey?" she asked.

"Now, that's more like it!" Floyd said with a grin as he reached for an apple crate standing on end by the stove, pulling it up to the table to sit down.

"No…here, you take this chair," said Shorty, shoving his own straight-back chair toward Floyd. "We ain't fixin' to eat or nothin'."

Shorty appeared to be a good many years older than Mary, who seemed much too attractive to be living with him. She had greeted Floyd with a smile and flashing eyes and I noticed right away that he seemed to be more interested in visiting with Mary than with Shorty. I wondered if that was because her style of dress was much more revealing and daring than what was worn by most of the local women.

Floyd moved from the apple crate to the chair as Mary placed a glass in front of him and poured him a drink from a nearly full bottle of whiskey. She went to the icebox and brought out a bottle of Coke and placed it on the table in front of Floyd. She then reached for a bottle opener on a small table by the stove and handed it to Floyd, who used it to flip the cap off the Coke.

Charles Ray was still standing just inside the kitchen and I was nearby, leaning against the door frame between the kitchen and the living room. Neither of us had said a word since our first greeting, but as Floyd turned up the glass with the whiskey in it and reached for the Coke with the other hand, Charles Ray whispered to me, "Come with me." He motioned toward the door at the back of the kitchen.

I followed him into the bedroom where there was only a bed on one side of the room and a gas heater on the other side with flames leaping above the top of the grates. The heater didn't seem to take much of the chill from the room.

We sat on the edge of the bed and talked about some of the things Charles Ray had experienced in his gypsy-like existence and about the arguments I got into with my brothers, which sometimes led to fights. Charles Ray also wanted to hear all about what it was like living out in the countryside, having farm animals, and going fishing and trapping. It seemed like we envied each other for the things we had seen and done. I longed to see the places in Texas where Charles Ray had lived, and do things like go to a rodeo. And Charles Ray wished for a large family and a life on a farm just like the one I had. We probably would have been trading one set of misfortunes for another, but then again, considering what a lonesome kid Charles Ray seemed to be, he might have been the winner in a trade.

We were both shy, but we had been talking up a storm and had gotten to know one another a lot better. It felt so different to be alone with him at his house rather than at school. We had never really learned much about each other at school, even though we were friends. But, after that day, I would consider Charles Ray my closest friend.

Meanwhile in the kitchen, Floyd, Shorty, and Mary continued talking and drinking until past noon. Cigarette smoke hung like a cloud in the room as all three of them smoked continuously.

Each time Charles Ray or I walked to the door and looked in on them, I could feel that Charles Ray was becoming more embarrassed by his mother's flirtatiousness and drinking. I could also see that Floyd was paying even more attention to her than he was previously, as Shorty was beginning to slump over on the table with a blank look on his face. The whiskey was beginning to get to all of them. This went on for another hour and by that time, Shorty was out cold, his head resting on the table between his folded arms.

I wished that Floyd would decide to go home. I tried to convince myself that there was nothing between Floyd and Mary except a mutual love of the whiskey, but I was not doing a very good job of it. I could hear the muffled voices and the laughter as they continued their drinking, completely ignoring Shorty.

By the time Floyd finally came to the bedroom door and instructed me to go to the truck, I was awfully hungry and tired and I didn't have to be told twice. I rushed through the door and headed outside. The rain had stopped, and Charles Ray followed me out into the yard and smiled as I turned to tell him goodbye. Charles Ray's smile seemed to show a kind of strained happiness that left a bit of the loneliness showing. I saw it or maybe I felt it, but one way or another, I knew it was there.

Maybe I imagined this because Charles Ray was living in an old rundown house in a place new to him, with his mother seemingly more concerned with good times than with his welfare, and a puny drunk of a stranger for a substitute father, who at that exact moment was sitting slumped over the kitchen table, passed out from too much drink.

"I'll see you Monday at school!" I yelled as I ran to the truck, climbed in and rolled down the window.

Charles Ray followed me, and walked up to the truck. "Okay," he said. "I'll teach you how to box. This man we lived with out in Texas used to be a boxer in the Marines and he showed me how." Charles Ray's boxing skills might have come in handy when James Johnson was bullying him at school, but James was a much older boy and Charles Ray was no match for him.

"Okay. I sure could use some teachin', with all them sorry brothers I got. They're always pickin' on me," I said, laughing.

We chatted more about what we would do during recess the next week and, ten minutes later, Floyd still had not come out of the house. I could see Charles Ray's nervousness and felt my own as we both occasionally glanced toward the front door of the house. In a few more minutes, Floyd and Mary came out onto the porch and, relieved that they had finally shown their faces, I waved goodbye to Charles Ray.

Floyd was in a happy mood as he started the truck and headed down the muddy road toward home. "That boy's momma ain't a bad lookin' woman, is she?" he asked.

I didn't answer Floyd because I didn't like what he had done. I couldn't help but think about Edra, who was just about the sweetest person in the world, and wonder what she would have thought if she'd seen the foolish way Floyd was carrying on with that woman.

Eleven

Winter 1952/1953

Floyd drove toward home for a couple of miles before he pulled the truck over on the side of the road, stopped and reached under the seat for his bottle of whiskey. As I watched him take a couple of swigs from the bottle, taking a deep breath between them, I was thinking that he had too much whiskey under his belt already. Floyd fumbled with the cap for a few seconds before making good contact with the top of the whiskey bottle. He finally got the cap tightened and then slid the bottle to the bottom of the paper bag before shoving it back under the seat and driving on.

Neither one of us was saying anything. All I had on my mind was eating because I was so hungry, and Floyd was busy trying to drive the old truck. It had about two full rounds of slack in the steering wheel and considering his impaired ability, courtesy of all the whiskey he had consumed, Floyd had his hands full just keeping the truck between the ditches on the wet, muddy road. On the one hand, I found humor in Floyd's struggle to drive the truck, but the thought that he might actually run the truck into a ditch made me uneasy.

Suddenly I remembered the Butterfinger I had stuck underneath Floyd's wool overcoat on the seat between us. I forgot about my fears as I tore the paper from one end of the candy bar and began eating it, glad that I had decided not to eat it at the store, and surprised I hadn't thought about eating it before that moment, since I was so hungry.

Floyd wrestled with the steering wheel with an ever increasing degree of uncertainty as he drove the next couple of miles to the Four Mile Post. That intersection branched out into five dirt roads, each of which led to a destination four miles away. It was four miles to the Alabama Landing on the Ouachita River down one road, four miles to Loco by another road, four miles to Haile on the road we had just traveled, and four miles to Linville by the other two roads.

Floyd turned right toward home and drove for a quarter mile before pulling over to the side of the road for another drink. While catching his breath between swigs, he looked over at me. "You want to drive on home?" he asked.

I grinned and shook my head, "I can't drive," I said in a tone of voice that hinted to Floyd that it was a dumb question.

"Aw, hell! Anybody can drive," Floyd said, waving his right arm out toward the windshield and pointing ahead at the road.

I just kept grinning and shaking my head no as Floyd insisted that I try it. My grin disappeared when Floyd opened his door, got out, slammed the door and came around to my side of the truck. "Scoot over, boy. You're fixin' to learn how to drive." The grin was on Floyd's face now.

Well, I guess I am! I thought as I slid under the steering wheel. I had to sit on the edge of the seat and stretch my legs to reach the clutch and brake pedals. I stretched my neck as far as I could and peered out over the hood. I would always remember the amusement and excitement of this moment, even though both feelings were to be short-lived.

With a little bit of instruction and a bunch of coaxing from Floyd, I prepared for the blastoff and boy, was it ever a blastoff! I pressed down on the accelerator until I could hear the engine revved up and then I eased out on the clutch until the truck began to roll forward and then, *bam!* I took my foot completely off the clutch and the truck lurched forward for about three neck-snapping leaps and then sputtered a time or two before the engine died.

Floyd voiced his disgust at this first attempt but gave me further instructions. "Ease out on the clutch until it gets to movin' good before you take your foot completely off the pedal," he said, "and hold the gas pedal steady."

The second attempt at takeoff was almost as rough, but I managed to keep the engine running and after settling down to an idle in low gear for a moment, I speeded up. After a couple of moments of going along like this, Floyd told me to clutch it and helped me make a shaky but successful shift into second gear.

For the next hundred yards, I stayed in second gear and fought the slack in the steering wheel as I veered from one side of the road to the other. Each time I was on the verge of coming to a complete stop, the truck would lurch forward, with Floyd yelling for me to gas it. By the time I reached my top speed of almost fifteen miles per hour, I had gained a little bit more confidence in my driving. The silly grin had returned to my face as I was staying more or less in the middle of the road.

Right as I was starting to feel good about my driving skills, I noticed a curve to the right in the road as it skirted the edge of a tree-and-brush-filled pond called Belchy Pond. In the middle of the muddy road were two deep ruts measuring about six to eight inches deep and a foot wide. The rest of the curve was covered with mud about eight inches deep. I had a feeling of impending disaster as I started into the curve and really began fighting the steering wheel.

When the truck reached the deepest part of the ruts and the sharpest part of the curve, it bounced from one side of the ruts to the other so fast that I could not catch up with the slack in the steering wheel. In effect, the truck was steering itself, with the front wheels bouncing off the walls of the deep ruts. Normally, when a driver's front wheels hit one side of the ruts, it would deflect the tires in the other direction. This didn't work in my case for two reasons—one, I didn't know how to drive and had no experience to guide me in keeping the front wheels in the ruts, and two, the extreme slack in the steering wheel made it impossible for me to react quickly enough in turning the wheel.

"Give it some gas and hold it in the ruts!" yelled Floyd, afraid that I was about to stick the truck.

This made me even more nervous than I had been already, and when I pressed the accelerator to the floor, all hell broke loose and the front wheels somehow jumped the walls of the ruts. Seeing the ditch coming at me over the hood of the truck, I totally abandoned my driving activities, and the force of the deep mud against the tires brought the truck to an abrupt halt almost squarely across the road. The truck was still in gear without the clutch being depressed, which caused the engine to shudder and die. For a second or two afterwards, there was quiet. I sat there smiling from embarrassment, feeling my face getting hotter by the second as I blushed.

Thoughts of what we had done that day passed quickly through my mind. I knew that Floyd was not going to congratulate me on a fine performance, even though he had been all smiles a couple of minutes earlier. But I had been tickled at the chance to drive, and thought I had done a pretty good job until the muddy curve got in my way.

My quick survey of the day up to that point was rudely interrupted by Floyd yelling at me, "Well, I'll be goddamned! Now look what you done gone and done!"

His tirade made me cringe and made me realize why none of my brothers wanted any part of Floyd's company. Now I knew why I was the only one of us boys that Floyd ever took with him on trips like this.

As Floyd continued yelling at me, he grabbed my arm and jerked me toward the passenger side of the truck. With the same motion, he raised up to crawl over me so he could get behind the steering wheel, but he had trouble getting over me because he was so drunk. This only made him madder and in his rage, he began kicking, his feet striking the truck's dashboard and the door.

As Floyd lay on his belly on top of me, I thought his weight was going to break my arms and I almost panicked. I began to squirm to get out from underneath him and managed to slide down onto my knees on the passenger-side floorboards. My back was toward the dashboard and my upper body was still over the seat. From the floorboards, I found myself in line with Floyd's kicking feet. He wasn't trying to kick me, he was just trying to get into position in the driver's seat.

The first kick caught me on my legs and it hurt, but the second one hit me squarely in the ribs, the force of the blow slamming me against the passenger door of the truck, and causing me to buckle in pain and fall to the floorboards. I tried not to cry, but the hurt and the fright were more than I could take, so the tears came anyway.

I saw the same rage in Floyd's eyes that I'd seen the day I had dumped the bike on him nearly two years earlier.

"Anybody that can't drive in goddamned ruts half a foot deep ought to have their ass kicked!" Floyd yelled as he prepared to start the truck. His face was tight and the veins in his neck were visible as he leaned over the steering wheel, listening to the motor slowly grinding several seconds before it cranked.

I didn't want Floyd to know that I was really hurting, so I quickly cut off the flow of tears with a strong effort at composing myself. I got up from the floorboards and sat on the edge of the seat, looking out the window of the truck's door on my right, so that Floyd could not see my face. The pain was intense but I resisted the urge to hold my side where Floyd had kicked me.

My mind was speeding along, reminding me of things I had heard from my older brothers concerning Floyd—things I could only vaguely recall. While I didn't remember an exact statement or incident, I did begin to realize why my brothers steered clear of Floyd most of the time. And I could feel myself getting ready to join them.

Floyd managed to get the truck straightened around in the road after much cursing and shifting from forward to reverse, spinning his tires, and racing the engine until blue smoke covered the entire area. Floyd glared at me as the truck finally rolled back into the ruts and he shifted into first gear for the last time as he resumed the drive toward home. Every time he would catch the slack in the steering wheel and send it spinning in the opposite direction, he would look over at me and glare.

"That's the last goddamned time I'll ever ask you to drive!" he said.

I clenched my teeth tightly and watched the woods passing by on my right. No longer scared and no longer feeling the pain, I thought, *You don't have to worry about that! You won't ever get the chance to ask me again!*

This incident with Floyd's truck was the beginning of a series of misfortunes that would befall my brothers and me at the curve at Belchy Pond.

A couple of years after my troubles there, Billy Joe was returning home after working the evening shift when the 1949 Mercury he had purchased shortly after being discharged from the Air Force left the road in this curve. It jumped the ditch on the inside of the curve, traveled a hundred feet or so, veered to the left, crossed the road and crashed into the ditch bank, throwing Billy Joe into the windshield.

When my brother came to his senses and realized that the car could not be driven, he began walking in the darkness toward home. He was aware that his face was cut badly and was bleeding a lot. After walking a quarter mile, a burning sensation in his left cheek caused him to reach up and feel it, and that's when he discovered a piece of the windshield glass embedded there. When he removed the glass, he realized to his horror that the glass had been impeding the flow of blood. By removing it, he released a steady stream of blood, causing him to rapidly weaken. By the time he reached the McCormicks' home a couple hundred yards further down the road, he could no longer walk due to his weakened condition from the loss of blood.

He somehow mustered enough strength to crawl the hundred and fifty feet from the road to the McCormicks' house, where he awakened and nearly frightened to death Mrs. McCormick who came to the door and failed to recognize the bloody face. Mr. McCormick came a few seconds after his wife had opened the door and upon seeing Billy Joe's face, he yelled for his grandson, who was asleep down the hall. Mr. McCormick had grown too old to drive and it was a stroke of real luck that his grandson happened to be there, had a driver license, and had his own car. The boy managed to get my brother to the clinic at Marion before he bled to death, but it was an extremely close call.

In later years after Terry Gene was grown, he had two automobile accidents in that same curve. One night he ran through a small herd of open range cattle sleeping in the road there, killing three or four cows, slightly injuring himself, and totally demolishing his car.

On another night some years later, he lost control of his car and began on the same course Billy Joe had taken, hitting the ditch on the inside of the curve. He fought the wheel and managed to keep the car between the ditch on his left that he had just crossed and the woods on his immediate right until he came to a halt, escaping injury on that occasion.

I would always approach that spot with caution and feel relief when it was behind me. When I thought back on it over the years, I would find it odd that this particular location was the scene of so much bad luck for my brothers and me. One or two incidents I could have dismissed as coincidental, but not four. In trying to reconcile it, I never could come up with a satisfactory answer, and I even began to wonder if some sort of evil spirit lurked there.

Twelve

Summer 1953

Time slowly rolled by and the dullness of the existence I shared with my brothers allowed our memories to grasp and hold forever certain events that might, at first glance, seem of little or no consequence and unworthy of storing for recall. But each of us children would have our own bank of memories to call on later in life—memories that would soothe in times of stress, bring sadness when sadness seemed to be called for, or bring a smile when there was a need for a reason to be happy.

The lazy days of late summer brought about stirrings in my brothers and me that seemed to arise from pent-up energy and move us to create some sort of entertainment designed to break the dullness. Sometimes on moonlit nights in late August, after the summer's heat and humidity had peaked and the temperatures began to decline ever so slightly, we would fan out across the stomp and into the field across the rocky road. (The stomp was the open area between our yard fence and the road that ran by our house, and was so named due to the free range cows or hogs that would come into that area at night to stand around or bed down, stomping their feet to try to shake off the horseflies that would bite their legs.) Or, we would walk up and down the road, but never so far as to tempt Shine or Lep, the hog dogs belonging to our neighbors, the McCormicks.

Both dogs looked vicious. Shine was a dark brown, brindled cur that had never bitten anyone but was known to raise the hackles on his back and stiffly sidle up to anyone who came too near to the McCormick yard.

His deep, rumbling growl would scare even the bravest of souls. Lep was a larger, gray-leopard-spotted cur with a glassy left eye, and could appear at times to be friendly. But he had actually bitten people on several occasions, striking silently from behind, always going for the heels.

Lep had learned to focus on heels the hard way, after experience had taught him that tusks could slice and rip. He had tangled with many a mad boar with scissor-like tusks snapping as he circled in close, instinct driving him in and out quickly to avoid being slashed. Once, a boar hemmed in by a briar patch had spun around quickly and ripped Lep's side, raking him from shoulder to flank. Were it not for Mr. McCormicks' experience in dealing with such matters, Lep would have been history. But he fought to live and he lived to fight, and became good at it. Now he knew that heels did not bite back.

Both Shine and Lep were well trained, and they would not venture more than a couple hundred feet from the yard without Mr. McCormick. That would only allow them to go as far as the gravel road that led by the house. There they would stand like silent sentinels, almost regal in the way they carried themselves, warning anyone walking by that trouble awaited them if they came too close. It was clear to see that they meant business, and my brothers and I knew and respected them.

The twins liked to stick together, and they would be the ones to set the tone and length of those forays into the moonlight. Some nights they would only sit on the roots of the giant pin oak tree that hung over the road across from the mailbox. There they would formulate their plans for the future, focus on their dreams of becoming sailors, and envision what it would be like to sail to all parts of the world, have a girl in every port, and learn to shoot guns as big as trees.

"As soon as we finish high school, we're getting our asses outta here!" they would say.

At other times, Mike and Ike would warn us younger brothers away as if they had some mysterious secret they did not want to share with us. They would wander across the field and then cut back across the road, climbing the rusty, dilapidated fence to gain access to the pasture. After their meanderings around the perimeter of the pasture, they might sit on the pile of old lumber and fence posts by the side of the barn and talk quietly for a while, and at this point they would usually allow us younger boys to rejoin the conversation.

Eventually we would all grow quiet and just gaze out over the farm bathed in the glow of the moon, listening to the night sounds made by the crickets and katydids, screech owls and whippoorwills. And we would argue over whether the whippoorwills were saying, "Jack married the widow" or "Chip fell off the white oak."

Once in a great while, a screech owl would appear in the pecan tree in the yard, making his eerie, screeching calls, and when this happened, one of us boys would rush to the house to tie a knot in the corner of a bath towel to make the owl go away and take his scary wailing with him.

Some nights would find the twins, Gerald, and me following our yard dogs, a mixture that included, at different times, hounds and dogs that were part hound, part feist or mongrel. (The mixture of the breed would change whenever Floyd traded out one of our dogs in hopes of getting a better squirrel dog, or with the appearance of unwanted puppies that had been dumped along the road by people driving through from who knows where.) There might be a rabbit chase, which would start with the cottontail circling the fields and end when it lost the dogs or the dogs lost interest. Or there may be an opossum treed by the dogs in one of the persimmon trees along the road. One of the older boys would climb the tree and try their best to shake the opossum out because we liked to watch him play dead, refusing to move until the area was clear of boys and dogs.

The days would pass with checking of the watermelons and cantaloupes for ripeness, or by pulling corn and hauling it to the crib in a ground slide pulled by the horse or mule, whichever Floyd happened to own at the time. Once the chores were completed, there were various homemade playthings that were occasionally utilized. One such thing was the spinning jenny. It was built on a knoll in the pasture, and consisted of a long oak pole attached to the top of a short post with a single large bolt serving as a spindle. This allowed two of us boys, one sitting on each end of the pole, to spin it around in a circle. The crudeness of the construction seemed to create regular breakdowns, which in turn created a challenge for Popeye or the twins who would try to repair it one more time before having to cut a new pole and bury a new post.

Most of the time when I would ride the spinning jenny, one of my older brothers was on the other end, and I almost always wound up being thrown off by too much speed or a sudden stop engineered by my bigger brother. Since it seemed like someone usually wound up flying through the air after being thrown off, we sometimes called it a flying jenny. But, we'd always be ready for another go-round, certain that the next time, we'd be able to hang on.

By that particular summer, I was almost eight years old, and felt I was ready to try the "go-devil" ride in the woods behind the pasture. Several years earlier, my older brothers had strung a long section of used cable through the trees. One end of the cable was attached about twenty feet up an oak tree and the other end was attached about seven or eight feet up another tree fifty feet away. The saplings under the length of cable were chopped down and a trail cleared near the lower end so we could stop ourselves at the end of the ride by dragging our feet on the trail.

Boards were nailed to the tree to make a ladder to the upper end of the cable and a small platform was built just beneath the point where the cable was tied around the tree. Popeye took a piece of flat metal bar from Floyd's scrap iron pile and formed a U-shape in the middle of the bar. Then he drilled a hole in the flats on each side of the "U" so he could bolt the bar to a white oak stake so we would have something to hang from while sliding down the cable.

Popeye and the twins would take turns climbing up to the platform, stake in hand. They would unbolt one side, slip the U-shaped clamp over the cable, bolt it good and tight, and take a moment or two to build up their courage. Then they would hang from the stake, jump off the platform, and go sliding down the cable, gaining speed as they got nearer to the low end. With someone riding it, the cable had enough slack in it that it would bottom out within fifteen feet of the far end and would be only five or six feet from the ground at its lowest point. At that point, the rider would stop himself quickly by dragging his feet on the ground.

By this point in time, the cable ride had been abandoned for a couple of years and the fast-growing sweet gums had grown up from the stumps where they had previously been cut down. You could never kill a sweet gum by chopping it down, for it would always sprout again from the stub. If you cut it off even with the ground, it would come back from the roots, and grow even faster than the time before, because the root system continued to grow bigger. The saplings were numerous underneath the cable and in the two summers they had been allowed to grow, some of them had reached a height of eight to ten feet. But, with the exception of those at the lower end, they still had quite a bit to grow before reaching the cable above them.

Whenever I would beg Popeye to let me try the cable ride in the previous year or two, I was warned to stay away from it. He told me that the ride had been abandoned because the slide stick had turned rotten, making the ride too dangerous. But, in late August, my chance came with the arrival of relatives from Richland Parish. Uncle Oscar and Aunt Mattie Smith, along with their youngest son, Poochie, who was sixteen, made the sixty-mile trip from their home to the Franklin farm for the first time in three years.

Poochie had ridden the go-devil before and was anxious to try it again. He was a star football player on his high school team, and he looked the part. He was six feet tall with broad, muscular shoulders, a crew cut, and a chipped front tooth he had gotten while butting heads with an opposing lineman the previous season. When Popeye asked about the tooth, Poochie told him what happened and then said with a wide grin, "I knocked his ass out as cold as a wedge!"

Poochie had spent just enough time in our house to receive hugs from Edra and Gramma, along with comments on how handsome and strong he looked before walking out the back door. He was headed to the huge muscadine vine between the back porch and the garden to search for the few remaining grapes on the thick vine.

Popeye, the twins, Gerald and I trailed behind Poochie, all of us in awe of him. First, there was his size and strength. Then there was the fact that he had been selected all-district in football, a fact which was brought to our attention by a newspaper clipping sent to us the previous winter by Aunt Mattie. Linville High School was too small to have a football program, so my brothers and I had never actually seen the game played, but we knew you had to be tough to play it, and if you made all-district, you had to be really tough! So we were proud to be cousins of Poochie.

"Hey, Popeye, have y'all still got that cable strung up back there in the woods?" Poochie asked while parting limbs and peering inside the muscadine vine, searching for grapes.

"Yeah, but we ain't rode it in a long time," answered Popeye. "But if you want to ride it, we can take a look at it. I know we'll have to build a new slide stick."

"Yeah, boy!" responded Poochie. "Let's do it! What do you call it? The go-devil ride, ain't it?"

"Yeah, it's a devil alright," said Popeye. He motioned for Poochie to follow him toward the gate leading into the pasture near the barn. "It's probably a rusty devil by now."

As Poochie followed Popeye, he was trailed by the twins, Gerald, and me. After crossing the pasture, we went through the gate, turned down the pipeline right-of-way and veered into the woods on our right a hundred feet further along. We made our way through the thick brush until we spotted the cable. Upon checking the slide bar, we found it to be aged enough by the weather that it had begun to rot through where the bolts held the U-clamp in place.

"We'll have to find a white oak sapling and cut a new stick," Popeye said to Poochie. "This one might hold me, but I know it would break if you tried it."

"Yeah, it probably would, and I ain't exactly ready to see if I can fly just yet!" said Poochie.

Popeye turned to the twins and said, "One of y'all run and get the ax while I find a good saplin'. Oh, and get some wrenches so I can take the old slide bar off the cable, too."

Mike and Ike immediately ran toward the pipeline which would lead them back to the house, and returned in less than ten minutes with the wrenches and Floyd's double-bit ax. By that time, Popeye had selected a white oak which was about two inches in diameter at a point six feet above its base.

Popeye used the ax to chop down the white oak sapling, keeping in mind the first thing we were taught about using the ax—always make sure the area behind you is clear of limbs or brush that could cause the ax to be deflected off course on your downswing. To clear the area, he bent the bushes near the sapling by pressing at their bases with the heel of his shoe. Using an ax without taking such precautions is very dangerous because the flat, narrow blade is easily deflected if it strikes something on the downswing. He had learned to be careful when using the ax, for he had used one many times in the days before the gas well was drilled on the farm. In those days, any of my brothers who were old enough to swing an ax got involved in gathering, chopping and splitting firewood.

He finished clearing the bushes from around the sapling and took the ax from Mike, immediately judging the correct distance to stand from the sapling before spreading his feet apart to gain a firm, balanced stance for swinging the ax. With a few quick strokes, he had the sapling laid over and then he cut through the trunk near the lowest limbs, leaving a pole about eight feet in length.

"Let's run to the shop and make a new slide stick," he said.

Poochie had approached after Popeye got the sapling cut. He had the old slide stick in one hand, the clamp in the other, and wrenches were protruding from both front pockets of his jeans. "Popeye, I hope you've got some more bolts. These two are rusty as hell. I don't believe I'd trust 'em."

"Oh, yeah," said Popeye. "Floyd's got all kinds of bolts in the shop so he can keep his damned old truck from fallin' apart!"

Poochie laughed, and said, "Well, let's go!"

Upon arriving at the shop building, Popeye placed the pole on a table, walked toward the back wall, and lifted a draw knife from where it was resting upon two nails. He walked back to the pole and placing the smaller end against his belt buckle, began peeling the bark off a two-foot section. After peeling all the bark off the end of the pole, he replaced the draw knife on the wall, grabbed a bucksaw and sawed off the ragged end of the pole. Then after placing both hands on the peeled section and visualizing hanging from the cable on it, he made a mark with a nail and proceeded to saw it to the proper length.

"What do you think, Poochie?" he asked, holding the cut section out toward his cousin.

Poochie gripped it with both hands and held it above his head, his arms fully extended, and said, "It's the right length, but it's too damned fat!"

"Shit, I know it's too damned fat! Let's just take it one step at a time, okay? I'm gonna fix that."

Popeye grinned as he took the short section of white oak from Poochie. He stood the stick on end on the workbench after finding Floyd's hatchet in the unorganized pile of tools lying there and with short downward strokes, he began hewing down the piece. He worked quickly, switching ends at regular intervals in order to keep the ends uniform as he worked them down to a comfortable size. When he was satisfied with the grips, he flattened two opposite sides at the middle so that he could attach the clamp, placed the clamp against the stick and marked where he needed to drill the holes.

Poochie had been sorting through a coffee can full of bolts and had picked out pairs of various sizes and lengths along with nuts and washers for them. "You ought to be able to use a pair of these," he said, placing a handful of bolts on the bench near Popeye.

Popeye picked up two bolts and held them against the stick, discarded those and picked up two slightly larger ones. "These will do just fine," he said, placing the stick in the vise mounted on the bench and turning the handle until the vise held the stick tightly.

He lifted a cigar box from a shelf above the workbench, took out a drill bit and placed one of the bolts alongside the bit. "Just right," he said. Then he chucked the bit into a hand-drill, walked back to the vise, and placing the rounded head of the hand-drill against his stomach so he could apply enough pressure, he began turning the hand-drill, drilling the two holes in a short time. He placed the clamp on the stick after releasing it from the vise, inserted the bolts and loosely attached the washers and nuts.

"Let's go! We're in business!" said Popeye, exiting the shop.

Poochie followed Popeye and I trailed shortly behind them. Across the pasture, at the edge of the woods, the twins stood and watched, waiting for us to return.

When we approached the site of the cable ride, Popeye walked down toward the lower end and looked back up at the cable and the platform at the upper end, saying, "We got to chop down them sweet gums."

"To hell with them sweet gums!" said Poochie. "Shit, I want to ride this devil! They'll probably make the ride more interesting anyway."

"I don't know," Popeye said slowly, clearly expressing his doubts about the wisdom behind Poochie's statement.

"Aw, heck! You worry too much! Let me take a slide!" said Poochie.

"Well, alright, but you better be careful. Them step boards we nailed to that tree may be rotten some and that platform is kind'a rickety too!" Popeye said. "Wait! Take these wrenches with you so you can tighten the bolts good and tight on the clamp. I still think you ought to let me chop down those sweet gums before you ride."

"Piss on it, Popeye! You ain't never had a linebacker bust your ass wide open, have you? Compared to that, this is gonna be a piece of cake!"

"No, and I don't plan on it happenin' any time soon, either," said Popeye, flashing that wide grin that had endeared him to so many people.

As Poochie began carefully climbing the board-ladder steps toward the platform above, Popeye began chopping down the bushes and saplings at the lower end of the cable anyway, swinging the ax as furiously as he safely could. He didn't want to hit the saplings himself at the end of his ride. He thought to himself, *Hell, I bet you're doing forty by the time you get to the bottom!*

Popeye had only cleared the brush from a ten to twelve foot strip under the cable when Poochie yelled at him from the platform, "Look out, I'm ready to slide!"

"Okay, let her rip!" Popeye yelled back as he stepped away from the cable, standing ten feet to one side. He looked around to make sure his brothers were clear of the area, and seeing that they were, he positioned himself where he could watch Poochie as he came down the cable.

Poochie was sitting on the edge of the platform with his legs hanging off, and as he inched closer to the edge, he tightened his grip on the slide bar, his hands close to the cable on each side. He bailed off the platform, letting out a loud Tarzan yell as the bar began its slide down the cable, quickly building up speed.

The Tarzan yell quickly changed to "Oh, shit!" as he realized that the cable was sagging down more than he had anticipated, and he saw that his legs were going to be passing through the tops of some of the taller saplings. As his speed increased, the downward arch in the cable carried him into the saplings, and with each slap of the limbs on his legs, he let out a grunt.

"Oh, Lord!" Popeye said softly as he saw that one sapling—the one he had been trying to get to before Poochie announced that he was ready to slide—was directly under the cable. He could see that the top of it would probably strike Poochie in the face, and that meant that his feet and legs were going to hit the sapling where most of the limbs were situated. He knew that the sapling would not bend or give much at that point, and Poochie was likely to suffer when he hit it. Little did he know just how much Poochie would suffer.

Poochie yelped loudly as he crashed through that last sweet gum, his legs passing on either side, causing the limbs to be gathered together as the tree passed between his legs. The insides of his legs took a pretty bad switching, and his crotch rode the sapling as it bent over under his weight and speed.

As soon as he had cleared the last sapling, Poochie released his grip on the slide bar and fell the last few feet to the ground, falling and rolling through the brush for several feet before coming to a complete stop. The bar slid on down the cable and bounced against the tree at the lower end.

Poochie was drawn up in a fetal position, groaning loudly and rocking back and forth slightly. "Ohhh, my balls!" he groaned. "Ohhh, my balls! Popeye, I believe I ripped my balls off!" He was almost in tears.

Popeye rushed over and knelt down beside him, resting his right hand on Poochie's shoulder. He quickly surveyed the many minor cuts and scratches on Poochie's face and arms and decided that, although he was really hurting badly, he was not badly hurt. "Poochie, I don't believe they're torn off, 'cause your britches ain't ripped and I don't see any blood."

Popeye was grinning slightly, relieved that Poochie was not really hurt, and aware that his remark would make him mad and make him laugh through his tears, which would make him get better quickly. He was right.

Poochie suddenly stopped groaning and turned over flat on his back, both hands still holding his crotch. "Why, you dirty son of a bitch! I ought to get up from here and kick your ass! Dammit, it ain't funny!"

Popeye laughed at this and stood up quickly, stepping backwards a couple of steps to be sure Poochie couldn't reach out and grab him. "I know it ain't funny. Hell, I had a hot grounder take a bad hop this spring when I was playin' third base and it like to have took my balls off when it hit me! But I ain't supposed to be tough. Hell, you're a football player! You're supposed to be like steel!"

Poochie grinned up at Popeye. The pain was quickly subsiding now, and he began to stand up, resting on one knee for a few seconds before getting up completely. "I am like steel, everywhere except for my balls!" He laughed and began checking out the scrapes and bruises, flexing from side to side at his waist and stretching his arms. "Hell, I'm okay. But let's cut most of them damned saplings down before you ride her, 'cause you couldn't survive what I just went through."

"Bullshit," said Popeye. "I could but I got more damned sense. I tried to tell you, but no, you wouldn't listen to me."

I watched and listened, smiling at the good-natured ribbing between the two cousins, and made up my mind that I would ride the go-devil as soon as they cleared the rest of the saplings underneath it. "Popeye, I want to go after you do."

Poochie looked around at me, saying, "Alright! Here's a little devil for sure!"

"No, I'd better not let you ride," said Popeye. "Edra would kill me if you got hurt."

"I won't get hurt! I'll hang on tight, I swear!" I replied, coming closer and looking up at Popeye with a pleading expression on my face.

"Aw, Popeye, let him ride it," said Poochie. "I'll stand under the cable at the highest part just in case he falls. I could catch him like a football, small as he is."

Popeye considered it for a few seconds, looking up at the cable. "Well, alright, but you better be damned sure you hang on tight."

"I will!" I said, my eyes flashing with excitement. I stood up a little bit straighter and looked around at the twins and Gerald. I knew the twins had ridden the go-devil, but I also knew that they both were still afraid of it to a certain extent. I didn't have enough sense to be afraid.

It only took fifteen minutes for the boys to get the saplings cleared out from under the cable—except for those under the highest part. After some discussion, they decided to leave them because there was no danger of hitting them and if the platform gave way, the limbs would help break the rider's fall. No one really wanted to fall ten feet into the treetops, but it appeared to be a lot less hazardous than falling twenty feet to the hard ground below.

Popeye decided that he would let me take my ride ahead of him, since he had to climb up the platform with me anyway in order to fasten the slide stick onto the cable. After I went down, Poochie would remove the slide stick and pitch it back up for Popeye's ride. My brother started me up the steps, staying right below me just in case a board broke. He cautioned me to be extra careful in climbing, saying, "I'm right behind you." But, the trip up to the platform went off without a hitch.

Popeye surveyed the situation when we got to the platform level and saw that there was not enough room for both of us on the platform at the same time. "Freddy Ray, you stand on that limb beside the platform and hold on tight to the tree. After I get the slide stick on the cable, I'll let you grab on to it and you can ease around to the front of the platform while I hold you."

I climbed onto the limb and stood up slowly, bear hugging the tree. My legs quivered slightly as I looked down at the ground beside the tree, thinking, *Boy, it looks like a mile to the ground!* I didn't look directly down again, but gazed down the length of the cable and thought of what fun the ride was going to be.

Popeye maneuvered around the tree onto the platform and lowered himself to a seated position slowly and gingerly, respecting the age of the weathered platform. He reached into his left rear pocket for the two end wrenches and proceeded to securely attach the slide bar to the cable.

"Okay, my little man," he said. "Ease your butt around here and hang onto this bar for dear life. Put your hands up close to the cable, the same distance from each side so you'll be balanced."

I did as I was told, and Popeye encircled my legs with his arms as he stepped onto the platform and asked me, "Now, you're sure you want to do this?"

I said "yeah" in a quiet voice that sounded more like talking to myself than my brother. My heart was beating fast but I was ready to go.

"Ready?" Popeye asked me.

"Yeah, let me get up on the front of the platform," I replied. Then I aligned myself dead center under the cable as I looked up at the slide stick, grabbed hold of it, tightened my grip and prepared to jump.

"Okay, I'm gonna turn you loose," said Popeye, and he removed his arms from around my legs. "You're on your own."

I took a deep breath and jumped from the platform. The slide bar grabbed the cable and seemed to hesitate twice in that first second or two before making a smooth, fast accelerating slide down the cable. I smiled as I realized that I had really done it, and the wind whistled in my ears as I watched the tops of the saplings passing beneath me and the freshly cleared ground passing in a blur.

I thought, *Boy, this is fun!*

The lower end of the cable was fast approaching. As I reached the low point, I realized that I was too light for my weight to make the cable sag down as it had with the older boys, and I was too short for my feet to touch the ground so that I could drag my feet and stop.

In those final couple of seconds, I panicked, and because I was going so fast, I couldn't bring myself to drop from the slide bar. As the tree came at me where the cable was tied, I realized that I was going to hit it at a speed that was slowed very little by the bottoming out of the cable. At the very last second, I saw that I had to try to protect myself, so I released my grip on the slide bar and tried to get my hands out in front of myself, toward the tree trunk, and barely managed to get them up in time to break some of my momentum.

Popeye was sitting with his legs hanging over the platform and now he was panicked, realizing that he had not put enough thought into letting me ride the go-devil ride. When he saw me fall and bounce off the tree, he leaned so far forward, he nearly fell off the platform and had to grab the cable to catch himself. He watched as I spun to my left and tumbled through the brush after hitting the tree. I lay still when I stopped rolling and Popeye leaned back against the tree and covered his face with his hands. He took a deep breath and looked back at me where I lay.

Poochie had watched my ride from his station underneath the high part of the cable, and had moved forward a number of feet while I had been above him. But now he realized he really should have stationed himself at the bottom of the cable to stop me when I reached there. He ran and knelt down beside me where I lay amid the brush the boys had thrown behind the anchor tree during their cleanup operation. The first thing he noticed was that the left side of my face was bleeding in strips where the bark lines of the tree had collided with my face. The knuckles on my right hand were skinned and my left forearm was badly scratched.

Looking up at Poochie, I was dazed, and sobbed softly.

"Little feller," Poochie said in a hushed, concerned voice, "you took a beatin' from that tree 'bout like I usually take in a football game. But I believe you're gonna survive."

My dizziness began to subside and I was more aware of the burning sensation from the cuts and scrapes inflicted upon me by the rough bark of the oak tree. "I'm alright now," I said, raising myself to a sitting position.

"Poochie!" Popeye yelled from the platform. "Did he break anything?"

"Naw, I don't think he broke anything," Poochie yelled back. "Well, he might have just broke my record for gettin' your ass busted!" He looked down at me and grinned that chipped-tooth grin.

Through the tears rolling down my cheek, I laughed a nervous laugh at Poochie's remark. I stopped crying and shakily got to my feet. After looking at my left arm, I wiped it on the side of my blue jeans and then pulled the front of my shirt up and wiped the blood from my face. I walked toward the tree and looked up at the slide bar and then up the cable toward Popeye.

"I'm gonna ride this son of a bitch again, and I'm gonna turn loose right there!" I said, pointing to the cable about fifteen feet from the tree. "I'll roll across the ground like a big Indian, but I ain't hittin' that damned tree again!"

Poochie laughed at the grit exhibited by me, his little cousin. "Boy, I'll tell you what. You'd make a helluva football player one of these days. You're a tough little shit!"

The twins and Gerald had been nearby watching the whole affair, and Ike and Gerald laughed at Poochie's statement. But Mike yelled at me, "You're crazy as hell if you plan to ride that damned thing again!"

I grinned shyly, and turned and ran to the ladder steps leading to the platform. I took another turn on the go-devil ride and didn't even have to rely on my plan to drop from the cable before I reached the tree. This time, Poochie was standing near the bottom of the ride, waiting to catch me. The summer ended with everyone healthy and still in one piece.

Thirteen

Fall, 1953

I had the healthy appetite of a growing boy, and when there was no food in the house, I would raid the garden, for vegetables were there for the gathering and they were plentiful. In some ways, our family was in the same boat as our animals and the hogs that roamed freely in the woods—our welfare was largely dependent upon nature's bounty.

The animals would be fat from the plentiful food supply by the time autumn rolled around, and with winter approaching, the food supply would dwindle and eventually it would virtually fade away. By the following spring, the animals would be lean and hungry, but would be rejuvenated by new growth in the new year.

The end of summer would find me round faced and for some reason, more tanned than the others in the family, but by the end of winter, I would be slim and pale. With so many mouths to feed, there seemed to be no way for Edra and Gramma to can enough vegetables to last beyond mid-winter. When the supply of canned vegetables was exhausted, the family's diet consisted mainly of wild game, which was scarce, and dried beans and peas, along with cornbread or biscuits.

Many times I would be too busy rambling around the farm when mealtime came, and by the time I did come into the house, there would be only a spoonful of peas or beans left in the pot. I would boil a cup of water in a frying pan, sprinkle corn meal into the boiling water until I had a mush, add the few precious peas or beans and a little salt, and make a meal of this.

The winter cold would creep into the house through cracks in the walls and floors, through broken windows shoddily patched with cardboard, and around ill-fitting doors. Those cold days of winter that I spent holed up in the house, trying to stay warm, would account for my pale skin.

It was around this time of my life that I began to understand the tension between Floyd and different members of the family. I heard bits and pieces of talk as Gramma and my older siblings discussed events that had occurred before my time—events that somehow seemed to be worse than any I had witnessed or endured. It was clear that Floyd had been mean to Grampa and hard on my older siblings. Even though Edra would listen, she seemed to fail to hear most of the talk, but even at that early age, I could recognize the sadness in her face—the love for Floyd mixed with an abhorrence of his misdeeds. And I could see her desire to protect us kids and her mother.

As things turned out, the ensuing years after Grampa's successful efforts to secure a pardon for Floyd brought endless battles between the two men. The verbal abuse Grampa endured at the hands of his son-in-law only worsened as the family increased in size and Grampa's health continued to deteriorate. In one particularly nasty incident, Grampa lost control of his bodily functions and had an accident, and Floyd got so frustrated he actually knocked Grampa over and gave him a cussing. Considering the way Floyd treated the man who literally saved his life—and returned to him his freedom!—I often wondered if Grampa regretted approaching the judge on his son-in-law's behalf.

I was aware that Floyd and Gramma hardly spoke to one another and when they did communicate, it was confined to short questions and curt replies. And as I mentioned earlier, the only flaw I ever observed in that precious woman's character was her willingness to voice to us children her dislike for Floyd and his actions toward us. Then I began to see with my own eyes the obvious disrespect my father had for my grandmother. It was hard to conceive of such disrespect considering all that Gramma did for us kids.

Gramma received a meager old-age pension from the state, and except for what she needed to spend on her medicine, she spent it all on us grandkids. Most of the money went toward the necessities of life, but she seemed to always have enough for those few special times that would arise as we were growing up. There was the time Myra Lou needed a new dress because her wardrobe had dwindled down to rags; there were the senior rings we wanted as we began to graduate from high school; and the pair of shoes for Gerald when winter came and the holes in his soles grew bigger than a half dollar.

Gramma's most valuable gift had nothing to do with her pension, and it was something she shared with all of us grandchildren daily—the gift of her love, understanding and guidance. She taught us to be good and honest and honorable, and her lessons were always sprinkled with a little wit to brighten our days. She was the one person who most influenced the lives of us Franklin children.

I was a curious boy and I watched, listened and remembered. I saw that all my brothers were afraid of Floyd, who seemed to harden as time went by. He offered no conversation to indicate that any of us children were anything more to him than persons to be used as needed and otherwise more or less ignored. He offered no lessons on life, no encouragement, no praise, only gruff orders that we would carry out at once, for fear of what might happen if we disobeyed.

I would watch Floyd's personality change when he came home drunk. Sometimes he would be in a mood that would drive us children to the far corners of the house, or outside the house to a place where peace could be found. Even when he was in a happy mood, none of us could really warm up to him because we knew the mercurial nature of his temperament and couldn't trust the momentary upswing.

Edra sank into the drudgery of her daily battle to keep up with the constant workload comprised of cooking, cleaning, washing and sewing piles of clothes. She insisted that we wear clean clothes to school, and rips and tears in our clothing had to be mended before we could wear them. She had great pride, and it drove her too hard and too long. My siblings and I let her sacrifice on our behalf, and Gramma, too, simultaneously seeing their sacrifice and failing to comprehend it. One day, we would become parents ourselves and only then would we truly understand the nature of sacrifice.

Edra had graduated from the wash pot and scrub board she once used for washing clothes to a wringer type washing machine, and no summer day was too hot or winter day too bitterly cold to keep her from standing at the washer on the back porch, washing the endless stream of jeans and shirts, socks and underclothes, dresses and overalls. She would feed them nervously through the wringer, jumping slightly and drawing away momentarily when a buckle on the overalls caused the rollers to separate and pop back together. And when an article of clothing gathered behind the rollers trying to force its way through, she would reach out and pull back on it quickly and then release her grip, afraid that somehow the wringer was going to grab her hand.

I noticed this and sometimes I would stand behind the machine and guide the wrung out clothes into the washtub for her, hoping to alleviate her nerve-wracking struggle with the wringer. With me helping, Edra didn't have to work both sides of the machine, and knowing I made her job easier gave me a sense of pride.

I would hold my hands under the article of clothing as it came through the wringer and play little games. For example, I would let the smaller or lighter articles of clothing feed through the rollers as far as they would go before hinging down and falling into the washtub when they were completely through the rollers. When it came to blue jeans, I liked to hold one finger under the first portion of them to come out of the rollers and see how far out beyond the rollers they would stay straight before they broke down in the middle. Then I would use my hands to help guide them, making sure they fell into the tub and not onto the floor behind or in front of the tub when they exited the rollers.

As spring came along, I continued to be aware of a gradual change taking place in me, a change that had begun over the past few months. I was trying to understand the changes happening to me but sorting through my thoughts required more maturity than an eight-year-old boy could muster. Something began to shift inside me over an incident that occurred during the previous September.

I had been in the back seat of the 1949 Chevrolet belonging to L.D. Turner, a man who Floyd spent some time with, usually drinking and rambling. L.D. was much younger than Floyd, and I sensed that they were a mismatched pair, not just on account of the age difference, but also the fact that L.D. was a single man.

My desire to be on the move was easily aroused, so I didn't really hesitate when asked if I wanted to go along. I was initially excited about the trip to Haile with Floyd and L.D. but on that Saturday morning, both men had been drinking heavily, and I felt uneasy about going off with them.

L.D. had asked Floyd to drive and he obliged, climbing into the driver's seat. As L.D. staggered around to get into the passenger side of the car, Terry Gene came out of the yard through the gate, and L.D. asked him if he wanted to go.

"Yessir!" replied Terry Gene, his eyes lighting up as he ran toward the car.

L.D. opened the rear door and Terry Gene climbed in, but as he began to sit down on the seat before pulling his feet completely inside, L.D. slammed the door. Terry Gene was unable to move quickly enough to save himself. His right foot nearly cleared the opening, but his toes were caught, and there was a dull crunching noise as the big toe on that foot was crushed by the slamming door.

I could almost feel the pain myself as I saw Terry Gene's face change from that excited expression to a pained grimace. The shock silenced Terry Gene for a few seconds and he sat with his mouth open, but no sound issuing forth. As L.D. realized what he had done and pulled the door open, freeing the foot, Terry Gene rolled over toward me and drew his knees up to his stomach. It was clear to see that he was in excruciating pain. He did not look down but reached with his hand and grabbed his toe, feeling the blood and the jagged edges of the toenail, broken open in the middle of the toe and protruding upwards. What he felt scared him and he rocked back and forth, crying silently, with me looking on helplessly, feeling deep sympathy for my brother but not knowing what to do.

Floyd got out from behind the steering wheel and came around the car to help Terry Gene. He said nothing as he reached into the car and lifted him out, lowering him down to rest his left foot and right heel on the ground. Floyd bent over and looked at the bloody toe and grunted softly. I slid across the seat of the car, dropped to the ground and stood beside Terry Gene, reaching for his left arm and holding onto it.

"L.D., you'd better just go on by yourself," Floyd said calmly. "I'd best take him in the house and doctor this foot up."

L.D. stepped backwards a couple of unsteady steps to give us room to pass. "I apologize. I didn't know his foot was still in the door. I apologize." The mournful look on his face did not touch me at all as I watched him stumble backwards and almost fall.

Floyd led Terry Gene away with me still holding onto his arm as he hobbled along slowly, dripping blood in the sandy trail toward the front door of the house.

Edra walked out the door onto the front porch and when she saw that Terry Gene was hurt, she rushed down the steps. "What happened?" she asked, moving Floyd aside and taking Terry Gene by his right arm. "I'll take care of him," she said.

"He got his foot caught in the door of the car," said Floyd, placing his hands on his hips and watching as Edra and I continued leading Terry Gene toward the steps leading up to the porch. Just inside the front door was a cane-bottom chair and Edra sat Terry Gene down in it, then ran toward the kitchen.

I stood next to Terry Gene's chair and watched through the door as Floyd walked slowly out to where L.D. was leaning against his car with his head hung down, his chin resting on his chest. As Floyd neared the car, I saw L.D. look up and begin shaking his head and gesturing with his hands.

I thought, *That drunk bastard! I just wish he would go on and leave!"*

Edra came from the kitchen and sat a dishpan half filled with water on the floor beside Terry Gene's foot and gently lifted his leg. Then she slowly eased the foot down into the water.

"Ohhhh! That hurts!" Terry Gene cried, jerking his foot out of the water, his body trembling slightly from the shock and pain. His misery seemed immeasurable as he extended his leg out, stretching as if he were trying to get the hurt foot as far away from his body as possible.

Edra kneeled down and gently wrapped a washcloth around Terry Gene's toes. "Let me run and heat some water. Warm water will make it feel better, and then when we get it cleaned up, I'll put some turpentine on it." She stood up, softly patted Terry Gene on his head, then rushed back toward the kitchen.

I was still nearby, awkwardly silent, but my presence was reassuring for my brother. I was still watching Floyd and L.D. out front. I saw L.D. get into his car and shut the door, still talking with Floyd through the open window.

I knew that L.D. was too drunk to drive and when I heard the car's engine turn over, I slowly walked to the porch so that I could watch him pull away. As the car began moving forward and turned toward the road, I saw our bicycle on its side in front of L.D.'s car. *Oh, no!* I thought, but I realized it was too late to do anything. L.D. was within ten feet of the bike, moving along in slow gear, and he never saw the bike.

After his car struck the bike and dragged it for a few feet, L.D. stopped, put the car in reverse, backed up and drove around the bike. He left it crumpled and beyond repair before pulling out to the road and driving away without acknowledging that he had run over our bicycle. My brothers and I had wished so hard for that bike and when it finally came into our lives, we somehow kept it going and shared that one bike between all of us, and now none of us would ever get to ride it again.

I watched that day unfold and tried to understand.

Two weekends later, Terry Gene's foot was healing nicely when he climbed up into the truck in preparation for the trip to Haile which had been so abruptly canceled a couple of weeks earlier. Floyd, who was drinking again, waited impatiently for Terry Gene to pull himself up on the seat, and then in his half-drunken, impatient frame of mind, he absentmindedly slammed the truck door hard because the doors of the old truck would not latch securely unless they were shut with force. And he caught Terry Gene's wounded toe in the door. The pain was more intense this time, and the crying was not subdued, and the damage to Terry Gene's toe was doubled as his excited anticipation of a trip for soda and candy was once again cruelly interrupted.

Once again, I was in the truck at the time, and almost sick to my stomach at the bloody sight. And somehow I felt the pain that Terry Gene was experiencing. Edra's treatment was once again quick and gentle, but the crying lasted much longer that day.

Terry Gene's toe would heal, but it would be disfigured for life. And there would be a place in my mind where that grisly memory would be stored to be used as another stepping stone that led me to mature earlier than most children. I would learn from those memories to always be more alert when I was around Floyd or any of his friends, and try to avoid them when they were drinking. That was the only way I knew to protect my brothers and myself from situations that might lead us into physical or emotional harm.

Fourteen

Winter/Early Spring 1954

N ear winter's end, Floyd began to think about spring and breaking ground for planting. It had really been on his mind since Christmas when Billy Joe came home on a furlough from the Air Force, and somehow managed to commit an error in judgment while at home that would affect the farm activities for quite some time.

After being away from home most of the past three years, Billy Joe was anxious to go rabbit hunting. Rabbits had been the family's main source of meat during the winter for as long as there had been a family, and the easiest, quickest and most efficient way to bag them was by spotlighting them at night.

All of my brothers old enough to handle a gun had at times strapped the carbide light to a miner's cap and walked the woods and fields, searching for that familiar red glow of a rabbit's eye reflected in the dim wavering light of the flame generated by the carbide gas as it burned and was magnified by the chrome reflector surrounding the flame. The shooting of the rabbits mesmerized by the light was not very sporting but shooting a .22 rifle did require skill and the necessity to provide food for the large family was simply a fact of life.

One night, as Billy Joe and Popeye set out across the pasture in hopes of bagging some rabbits, Billy Joe caught the distant glow of an eye with an unfamiliar color. He stopped walking and watched for a moment, intrigued by the unusual movements of the eye reflected in the light. It moved in jerking motions just above the ground near the fence separating the pasture from the garden.

Billy Joe quickly decided that this was a fox that had been approaching the Chinese tallow trees at the rear of the yard, trying to catch one of Edra's chickens roosting throughout the lower limbs of the trees. He assumed the erratic movements were the result of the spooked fox partially blinded by the light and caught against the garden fence, unable to get away.

"That's a fox, ain't it?" Billy Joe whispered to Popeye, who was standing close behind him and looking over his shoulder, trying to distinguish some form behind the eye.

"I don't know," replied Popeye softly. "I can't see nothin' but his eye, but I think it is."

"Well, hell, it's got to be!" whispered Billy Joe, as he slowly brought his rifle up to his right shoulder and aimed it at the eye. He waited for the forward eye movement to stop and when it did so, he fired.

The crack of the rifle rang out in the night and echoes bounced off the wall of trees in four different directions. Before the echoes subsided, the reflected eye jerked upwards as high as a man's head and held steady for a second or two. That was just enough time for Billy Joe to panic. He was completely bewildered by what he was seeing. What was this thing he had shot at?

With a leap it was off and running, and Billy Joe's heart leapt also, for there was a pounding of hooves. He realized then that he had shot at Nell, the family's solid black mare, the horse that Floyd used for all his plowing and we boys rode for pleasure. Now he understood why he could see nothing but black all around the eye reflected by the light. Nell had been grazing and had she not been so accustomed to the hunting light, she might have raised her head to watch. Had she done this, she would have prevented Billy Joe from mistaking the reflection of her eye for that of a fox's eye.

"Oh, shit!" said Billy Joe as the horse ran toward the far side of the pasture. "Damn! I hope I didn't hit her!"

"I don't guess you did, the way she's runnin'!" said Popeye.

They stood listening as the hoof beats circled around the pasture. Nell came back into sight as she neared the barn, which was not far behind them. She ran at almost full speed until she was directly in front of the barn, where she stopped abruptly. Billy Joe's stomach began to churn as he heard the wheezing sound and saw the horse falter and begin to lose her balance. She fell to the ground and lay over on her side, slowly kicking with her legs extended straight out from her body.

Billy Joe's shot had hit the horse just above the eye and proved to be fatal. He realized that he had really been negligent in his actions, failing to follow a rule of night hunting he had often stressed upon his younger brothers, namely that you don't shoot if you don't know what you're shooting at. He understood too late that, if he had just waited long enough, Nell would have raised her head and he would have known it was the horse. Little did he realize just how many problems would follow as a result of this accident.

Floyd didn't lose his temper; he just fussed at Billy Joe and made it clear he was going to need to replace Nell at his own expense. There were two things that may have accounted for Floyd's uncharacteristic self-control. First of all, he was probably afraid to be too mean to Billy Joe who was now a grown man. And secondly, good plow horses or mules were fairly plentiful and locating a good one did not pose a big problem. My brother's pay for the next two or three months would be sufficient to replace Nell, and he promised Floyd to send whatever it took, once he got back to his base in Minnesota.

Floyd, in his eagerness to replace his plow horse, bought the first mule a local horse trader brought for him to try. It was a young, strong mule that had been trained to plow but had never been put to the real test in the fields. For this reason, the price tag was only sixty-five dollars and this seemed to Floyd a deal too good to pass up. And for the first few days, it seemed that Floyd had made a good deal. During this time, he kept plenty of grain in the feed trough and the mule seemed to be a big pet, following close behind Floyd when he made his daily trip to the barn to put out the feed.

The problems started after the mule became accustomed to the place, for that's when Floyd cut the grain supply to a small daily portion, causing the mule to have to scrounge for something to eat in the close-cropped grasses of the small pasture. It wasn't long before the weeds beyond the ragged wire fence enclosing the pasture began to look good to the mule, and it also wasn't long before he figured out that he could jump over the fence at some of its low points.

The first time Floyd came home from work and found the mule munching away along the edges of the woods outside the pasture, he knew he had a problem that had to be dealt with quickly. He put some grain in a bucket and led the mule back into the pasture before stretching together scraps of barbed wire along the top of the fence where the mule had jumped it. The next day, he came home with a yoke he had built at work from steel rod formed into the shape of an oval. The yoke was large enough to be placed around the mule's neck, with a twelve-inch-long rod welded at the bottom front of the yoke where it would point straight ahead. It was designed to hook into the net wire and stop the mule when he reared up against the fence, preparing to jump over.

Floyd was sure his problems with the fence jumping mule were over but the following day, he found the mule out again. Upon inspecting the fences, he found a section at the top where a hole had been torn by the yoke as it ripped through the rusty wire.

Floyd cursed the mule and once again stretched barbed wire over the opening, the cold wind nearly freezing him while he was patching the fence. Before he went into the house for supper, he took a plow line, looped it around the mule's neck and led him over to the side of the barn where he tied the rope around the end of a heavy railroad crosstie. He then took the rope from around the mule's neck and tied it to the iron yoke, leaving about ten feet of rope trailing back to the crosstie.

"Now, let me see you jump a fence with that draggin' behind you, you son of a bitch!" he muttered to the mule, grinning with satisfaction, sure that he had eliminated the problem.

I had been close by, watching with great curiosity and getting colder and colder, so I was glad to see Floyd head for the house.

The next afternoon when the school bus dropped us off after school, my brothers and I were anxious to see what the mule had done that day. We had made bets as to whether the combination of the yoke and the crosstie would keep him inside the pasture.

I was sure that Floyd had found a solution and when I saw that the mule was still in the pasture, I bragged to the twins who had been skeptical, "I told y'all so!"

Floyd was also pleased when he arrived home from work and found that his rigging had worked. But his satisfaction was again to be short-lived, for the very next day the mule jumped the fence once more. This time the metal rod tore a short section of the fence and the mule dragged the crosstie behind him, leaving an opening wide enough to drive a truck through.

Mules were naturally stubborn and Floyd was naturally mule-headed, and the two were providing an almost daily attraction for my brothers and me as we discussed the latest twist and debated as to what might follow.

Mike was particularly amused. "The only way Floyd could ever keep that mule in would be by buildin' a fence six feet high, and if it crosses his mind, he probably will," he said.

It never crossed Floyd's mind. What did, however, was a type of imprisonment and that was a ball and chain for the mule. Floyd came up with an iron ball that weighed about fifteen pounds and he welded it to an eight-foot length of heavy chain. He formed a clamp from a steel flat bar and welded it to the other end of the chain. The day he brought home the ball and chain, my brothers and I laughed. But Floyd's face bore a look of confidence like we had never seen before, and when he bolted the clamp around the mule's right front leg just above the hoof, we understood that this was it. There would be no way for the mule to jump now.

The mule dragged the ball and chain around the pasture for two days, moving slowly and painfully. On the third day, Floyd knew he had won the battle, for that afternoon the mule stood near the middle of the pasture and by nightfall had moved only a very short distance, if any. But when Floyd looked out across the pasture the next morning and the mule was still standing in the same spot as the night before, he went to investigate. He found that the steel clamp had worn the hide off the mule's leg, and was chewing into its flesh, leaving a bloody circle just below the mule's fetlock.

"Shit!" said Floyd. "I never thought about the clamp chewin' the son of a bitch's leg off!"

So off came the ball and chain, and Floyd mopped creosote dip on the leg until it healed enough for the mule to run away when he saw Floyd coming toward him with that bottle of misery that burned like fire when applied to the wound. The mule had learned that Floyd meant trouble and he intended to stay clear of him if he could.

There was to be one final blow in this match of stubborn man versus stubborn mule, for when Floyd went out to try and catch the mule one day to see if the foot had completely healed, the mule ran away across the pasture. Floyd could not get closer than fifty or sixty feet, even with a bucket of feed, before the mule would trot off again.

After chasing and cursing the mule for a while, Floyd walked toward the barn, steadily cursing. Standing just inside the yard watching were the twins, Gerald, Terry Gene and me, trying to hide our amusement.

"Ike, go get my goddamned shotgun and a handful of shells!" yelled Floyd.

Ike went at once to the back door and disappeared into the house, going straight to Floyd's bedroom, where the sixteen-gauge single-barrel shotgun stood against the wall in a corner. He picked it up and laid it across the bed, then turned to Floyd's homemade, two-drawer cabinet by the bedside. He pulled open the bottom drawer and grabbed four shells, leaving the drawer open as he picked up the gun and ran out of the house. By the time he reached the fence where Floyd stood waiting and handed him the gun and shells, he was almost out of breath.

Looking at the shells and seeing that they were buckshot, Floyd asked, "Couldn't you find some squirrel shot?"

"That's the only ones I saw," Ike said meekly, afraid to tell Floyd that he had grabbed the first shells he saw.

"Good!" said Floyd. "I'll teach that goddamned mule to run from me! If I kill the son of a bitch, I won't have lost nothin'!"

He broke open the shotgun, put a shell in the chamber, and with the butt of the gun under his right armpit, he flipped the gun upwards and then reversed directions, causing the barrel to swing up and latch. As he stuck the remaining shells in the front pocket of his overalls and walked toward the mule, the brothers looked at one another nervously, unsure of what Floyd was really going to do.

"Ike, why in the hell didn't you get squirrel shot?" Mike whispered to his twin. "Hell, he's gonna kill him if he shoots him with that buckshot!"

"There weren't no damned squirrel shot!" Ike replied, plainly agitated by the tone of Mike's question. "Besides, Floyd ain't gonna shoot the mule."

We watched Floyd walk toward the mule but when he got within fifty yards of him, the mule turned and began walking away. Floyd cursed again, brought the gun to his shoulder and fired.

When the buckshot struck him, the mule's rear end quickly jerked forward and he jumped and ran a few yards, looking back with a wild look in his eyes, his ears laying back against his head, then standing up, then laying back again.

Floyd walked slowly toward the mule, speaking loudly to him. "Whoa," he called. But the mule began to walk away again.

Once again, Floyd quickly reloaded and fired. This time, the mule was obviously wounded in the left rear hind quarter, for the boys could see several areas where the shots had penetrated the hide and blood was beginning to ooze.

The mule ran a couple hundred feet, then stopped, frightened and confused. He looked around, over his right shoulder, then swung his head around and looked over his left shoulder at Floyd, who was reloading his shotgun and still walking toward the mule.

Floyd yelled again in a loud voice as he walked closer to the mule, "Whoa!" The mule allowed him to get a bit closer this time before he began to walk away rather unsteadily.

"You son of a bitch, I'm gonna catch you if I have to kill you to do it!" Floyd said through clenched teeth as he fired on the mule once again.

I watched in pain as the mule's body jerked abruptly when the buckshot pellets tore into his rear end. I felt certain the mule would fall over dead and I watched silently, my hands tightly gripping the top strand of the fence wire.

Floyd walked slowly toward the mule, calling out "whoa" in a quieter tone as he got nearer. The mule did not walk away any further but stood there quivering as Floyd walked up to him and rubbed the side of the mule's head. "Now, by God, I bet you don't run from me anymore!" he said before looping a hay string he pulled from the pocket of his overalls around the mule's neck and leading him toward the barn.

I suddenly realized my fingers were hurting from clutching the fence wire so tightly. I released my grip and turned around to speak to Ike but there was no one there. As I turned toward the house, I could see my brothers peeping from a window and behind them stood Gramma and Edra.

At bedtime, Edra made her rounds by the boys' rooms. "It's bedtime. Y'all need to go pee." She herded us toward the front door.

The outhouse was far from the house, behind the garden fence, in order to keep any unpleasant odors from drifting to the house when there was no lime to pour into the pit. In addition to the trail being virtually impossible to traverse in the darkness, there was the ever present danger of stepping on snakes that came out at night during much of the year. So we had become accustomed to merely walking to the edge of the field where the light cast by the bare windows from the house was sufficient for us to see where we were going, and there we would relieve ourselves.

On that night, my brothers and I shut the door behind us and stood at the edge of the porch, Terry Gene beside the step, me holding onto the post supporting the roof near the step, and then Gerald, Ike, and Mike. A good deal of light was shining through the window and onto the porch, thanks to the lack of curtains and the bare bulb hanging at the end of a wire suspended from the ceiling in the living room behind us.

Ike unzipped his pants and looked down the line at his brothers. "Instead of goin' out yonder, why don't we just stand here on the porch and have a pissin' contest? I'll just bet I can out-piss all of y'all!"

The rest of us reached for our zippers in unison and stepped to the edge of the porch, each of us declaring ourselves the winner in advance. Everyone's voices combined and eliminated the chance of recognizing any one individual—except for me. I always seemed to be slow in voicing my thoughts but quick in initiating action.

"I'll bet you can't beat me!" I piped up as I stood with goober in hand, ready for the start.

And the contest was on, with us five boys streaming it out across the dust in the yard in front of the porch. Poor Terry Gene could barely get it over his feet, but he was only five years old, so he really shouldn't have even been in the contest. The rest of us were giving it all we had, standing on our tiptoes and leaning out as far as we could, and our streams were fairly close together in distance. I hooked my left arm around the post to keep from falling off the porch, for it was four feet down to the ground and I was not quite that tall.

Each of us declared ourselves the winner again before we were through except for Terry Gene, who was still dribbling beside the step. But I took a deep breath and arched my back, leaning out, holding onto the post at arm's length with my left hand and holding my goober tight in my right. And I raised little puffs of dust a full three feet further out than any of them.

"I'm the champeen pisser!" I said, exhaling loudly after the exertion required for my victory feat, and I laughed at the others as my stream slowly trailed through the dust back to the edge of the porch and stopped completely.

"No wonder!" said Mike. "With that little cigarette peter of yours, you ought of have lots of pressure!"

The others laughed at Mike's remark, especially Terry Gene, who pointed at my crotch and yelled, "Lucky Strike!"

"Ahhh, y'all are just jealous 'cause you ain't got the power like I got!" I said, walking to the far end of the porch as the others, still laughing, began trailing back into the house. I stood there for a few minutes looking out toward the pasture. In the darkness, I thought I could see the fence, but I was not sure. I wondered about the mule and wondered if it had died since nightfall.

My concern overrode my fear of the darkness and I walked to the other end of the porch and went down the steps. Making a wide circle in the yard to avoid stepping into the wetness produced by the contest, I walked carefully toward the pasture fence, feeling the ground with my bare feet before placing my weight down for the next step.

When I got to the fence, I whistled softly and waited a moment for a response. When there was none, I whistled softly again, straining my eyes and ears in the darkness and silence for any sign of the mule. I decided that my fears were founded. The mule had either died or was dying. After another minute or two, I started getting nervous because of the darkness and turned to walk back toward the house. But just as I turned to go, I heard something in the pasture. I turned back and strained to see what it was, and out of the darkness loomed a large figure, and there was the mule, moving very slowly toward me.

I whistled softly again and the mule walked to the fence and stuck his head over it, his muzzle touching my chest curiously. "Hey, boy! How you doin'?" I asked, thrilled to see the mule still moving about.

The mule stood quietly as I stroked the side of its head and along its neck as far as I could reach. And as I stood there in the near total darkness with the wounded mule, I began to realize that Floyd had exercised his power of ruling by fear that day, and he had done so in a way that was more cruel than I could have previously imagined.

"Good boy. You're gonna be alright," I said as I patted the side of the mule's head one last time. And he was alright—to a point. The mule did recover from his wounds but not from his fear of Floyd. He never ran from Floyd again, but would stand and quiver slightly as Floyd placed the bridle around his neck and led him to the barn to be harnessed.

I was halfway back to the house when the front door opened and a light flooded a long strip across the front yard. I saw Edra step through the front door and look around across the yard, holding her open right hand beside her face to cut down the glare from the light inside. "Freddy Ray," she called, "you better get back in this house, and right now!"

Fifteen

Spring/Summer/Fall 1954

S pring passed and the planting was done and the few acres of corn, peas and beans took their normal place in the scheme of things, as there was plowing and hoeing to be done, and then the picking of the peas and beans, and later the pulling of the corn. Special attention was paid in the planting and care of the watermelons on the terrace row—the one long row curving along the edge of the breakover into the bottomland. Floyd prided himself on his ability to raise good melons.

All things continued as they had in previous years— the heat and humidity, the endless drudgery for Edra, the bickering and fighting among us boys, the unwavering sweetness and serenity of Myra Lou, and the wisdom that came with age that was being passed down to us children by Gramma. Then there were the weekends tainted by Floyd's drinking and unpredictable attitude and actions, followed by weekday evenings when he was either gruff or silent, usually the latter.

The personalities of my brothers and me changed drastically whenever Floyd arrived at home after work. We changed from outgoing individual personalities to a group which had as its joint personality somberness and silence. We walked lightly around our father and unhesitatingly tended to chores as directed. Myra Lou helped Gramma and Edra with the cooking and housework and then she returned to her books, in order to maintain her perfect grades in school.

I continued to help Floyd with his welding projects, such as building gates and pipe fences, swing sets and picnic tables. The fences were built at the homes of various people who contracted Floyd, but the remaining work was usually done in the shade of the mulberry tree next to the shop building. I enjoyed the fence-building jobs at the various locations because they gave me a chance to get away from home and I was a real help, for I was nearing nine and strong for my age. I even learned to spin the crank and start the used welding machine Floyd had purchased, and I was especially proud of this accomplishment for I had seen grown men who had great difficulty in starting the engine with the hand crank.

I worked silently for Floyd, who only spoke when there was a need to instruct. Ours was a strained partnership beneficial to us both. Floyd always needed someone to hold the pipes or iron when tack welding the pieces together, and I cleaned the welds for him and fetched materials and drinking water. As for me, I was motivated by the joy I derived in seeing functional things materialize from the iron and scrap pile beside the shop building. I intently watched the welding and burning through a spare welding helmet or goggles, studying the technique in each process. Although I was unaware of it at the time, I was recording everything I saw for my own use in later years.

I had come to harbor a distrust of Floyd and even a dislike for him, but something I couldn't understand or explain kept drawing me toward him when he was working at home. We never talked together about anything at all. I directed a minimum of necessary questions at Floyd and they were met with a minimum of instructions, and this so-called conversation concerned only our present projects.

There was also a sadness that began to creep into my mind, arising from the awareness that I really knew nothing about my own father except for that which I had glimpsed from across the chasm of his indifference. Over time, I began to realize that I was being cheated. I thought about my schoolmates and there was not a single one that I could think of that harbored a hint of dislike for their fathers. I dwelled on these thoughts and decided that my friends were more fortunate than I. Fear began to build in me because I felt as though I was in charge of my own destiny, and I could not fully understand how I was supposed to handle this responsibility.

There were other changes taking place in the family, as well, and they affected everyone. One change had begun two years prior to this year, on December 23rd, 1952, when Edra gave birth to Ricky, the twelfth child born by her and the first who was delivered in a medical clinic instead of at home. Elizabeth had helped Gramma with her midwife duties with several of her younger siblings' births, and after Ricky's birth, Elizabeth persuaded Edra to have an operation to stop the perpetuation of this risky marathon. She had also been the main force responsible for Ricky's birth taking place at the Marion Clinic because nursing school opened her eyes to the very real dangers of having children at home.

The following couple of years were perplexing times for the whole family, for no one (except perhaps Gramma) seemed to realize or understand what was going on within Edra's body and mind. Reflecting back in later years, I concluded that my mother was probably going through menopause at that time of her life, but while it was happening, no one in the family was aware of the perfectly legitimate cause of her vicissitude. I think that the change of life Edra was undergoing might have sparked Floyd's anger with her at times. His hair-trigger temper led to an event that would have lifelong repercussions for some members of the family, especially me.

It was late autumn of 1954 and there was a chill in the air. The day had dawned without a hint of the series of events the day would bring—events that would haunt me for years to come. It was nearing midday and I was alone in the yard at the side of the house, absorbed in my thoughts. I had just returned to the yard from meandering around the field to the west, following the trails of field mice for amusement, those trails now exposed by the thinning of the grasses as they went dormant for the winter and began to shrivel up.

Terry Gene came running up to me with a wild, frightened look on his face. "Floyd's killin' Edra!" he blurted out.

Shocked, I spun around, directly facing my brother. "What are you talkin' about?" I knew this couldn't be true, but Terry Gene appeared to be truly terrified.

"He's beatin' her up! In the house there!" he said, pointing in the direction of the back door. He was crying now. I didn't know if my brother was simply letting me know what was going on or expecting me to do something about it, but the look in his eyes let me know that I needed to see for myself what was happening, and quick.

I ran for the back porch as hard as I could, jumping from the ground completely over the steps up onto the porch, and past the screen door that hung wide open, its spring return hanging loose. I pushed open the kitchen door and ran inside just in time to see Gramma and the twins back away from the door leading into the large bedroom adjacent to the kitchen. There was a commotion in the bedroom and they stepped toward the door again, peering through the open door into the bedroom. Gerald followed them, peeping around from behind Gramma. Myra Lou was over at the far end of the kitchen, beyond the door, leaning against the logs that formed the wall behind her, with both hands covering her face, trying to blot out what was going on around her.

I crowded in between the group at the side of the door and stepped directly into the opening. Just as I did, Floyd slapped Edra viciously, knocking her across the room, where a bed stopped her and she fell across it, crying and moaning. Cursing, Floyd reached for her hand and pulled her roughly to her feet.

Something had to be done and done quickly, for my mother was in serious trouble. My first thought was about Popeye, who would have been able to put a stop to this terrible situation. But he wasn't there. He had left school the previous afternoon with his classmate, James Wall, and was planning to spend the weekend near Sterlington at the home of James's family.

I looked around at the frightened faces behind me and realized that they were all too scared of Floyd to do anything. At that point, I resolved to do anything within my power to stop Floyd. In coming years, I would marvel at my reaction to this emergency.

I quickly looked around the kitchen and saw nothing that I could use as a weapon of force, so I ran for the back door, knowing that I could find a club of some sort outside. When Ike saw the look on my face, he knew I was not running from the scene out of fright. He followed me out of the house and found me at the side of the house to the right of the back steps, searching among the boards and clutter protruding from underneath the house.

With a strange, curious expression on his face, my brother approached me, asking, "Boy, what are you doin'?"

"I'm lookin' for something to kill Floyd with before he kills Edra!" I replied, looking up just long enough to see that strange expression on Ike's face. Then I did not look at him again.

Then I saw it—a brick just underneath the house. It was a heavy, solid brick, something I knew I could throw with force and accuracy. I fell to my knees, grabbing it up with both hands. I had already forgotten Ike was even there as I ran back into the house.

As I approached the door to the bedroom, I could hear cursing from Floyd and sobs from Edra, and this made me even more determined to do what I knew I had to do, and that was rescue my mother. I held the brick behind my back and eased myself through the doorway. With my back to the wall, I made my way to the wall opposite Floyd, who now stood facing away from me.

Gramma appeared in the doorway and watched as I began to slowly inch my way forward, closely watching Floyd's back. She was too frightened to enter the room, fearing that she too would be beaten, so all she could do was stand there, hoping and praying that I would look her way. And for a split second, I did look at Gramma, with a purposeful look that belied my age. When our eyes met, she frowned at me, shaking her head quickly from side to side, motioning for me to come back out into the kitchen and out of the danger in which I was placing myself.

I ignored Gramma, and did not look her way again. I was almost halfway across the large room, concentrating on the back of Floyd's neck and the base of his skull, for something told me that was where I needed to aim for the brick to do the most damage. I knew that I could throw that brick with accuracy and I knew that I could kill him if I could get a couple of feet closer and throw with all my might. But I also knew that I had to get closer for my aim to be true, for there would be no second chance.

I was scared but I intended to try to kill Floyd with the brick. Every bad thought I had ever had about my father merged into an intense hatred like I had never before felt for this man who stood over my mother, threatening to strike her again. Edra was recovering from the previous blow and her spirit forced her to attempt to strike back at Floyd. I could see the tears streaming down her face and moved sideways so that Floyd's back blocked my view of my mother. I wanted to avoid seeing her tears, and I also wanted to make sure that there was no danger of the brick hitting her if, by chance, my aim was not true and I missed Floyd.

I was completely unprepared for what I saw next, for out of the corner of my eye, I caught sight of someone coming through the door. I looked over to see Ike with a three-foot-long piece of one-inch diameter steel pipe held behind his legs and back, the end of it almost dragging on the floor. Ike made his entrance into the room the same as I had, walking sideways and moving along the wall until he got around behind Floyd.

Up until this moment, I had thought that all my brothers were as frightened as I was, and that I was simply crazy for being in such close proximity to Floyd. But with Ike's actions, I saw pure bravery—something I did not know my brother possessed until that very moment. And it gave me the confidence I needed to carry out my mission. Ike would not have to participate in my mission, but I was glad he was there.

At that point, Floyd struck Edra again, knocking her back against the wall and against a flimsy, gas space heater. The asbestos backing behind the flames flaked off and into the flame as the heater slammed against the wall, causing the blue flame to change to an eerie orange color, wavering around the pieces of asbestos that fell down on the gas pipes. By some miracle, Edra did not get burned, but the orange glow of the flames seared its way into my memory and I never forgot the image.

The swiftness of it all left little time for reasoning, even if I had been capable of reasoning at that age. I knew that I had to rescue my mother as I glanced quickly toward those frightened faces peering through the door.

I extended my arm and brought the brick up behind me, taking one last step toward Floyd in order to make sure my aim would be true. And with total concentration on the base of Floyd's skull, I prepared to throw the brick as hard as I had ever thrown anything in my life.

Suddenly, out of the corner of my eye, I caught a glimpse of something moving, distracting me for an instant, and there was that steel pipe coming down in a swift arc toward the back of Floyd's head. Ike had reacted a split second faster than I had—but the pipe that Ike was holding struck a heavy wire just before it would have hit Floyd's head. The wire had been strung across the room for Edra who used it to hang clothes to dry on rainy days.

The force of the blow on the wire jerked the fencing staple loose from the log where the wire was nailed in the nearby corner of the room, uprooting it with such force that it flew by like a bullet. I would always remember the whizzing sound of the staple as it flew by my face and through the air, barely missing me.

The wire fell across Floyd's back and, as he began to turn to see what caused the commotion, the recoil of the wire about him caused him to throw his arms up in front of his face to protect himself from the whipping wire. That little bit of time was all that Ike and I needed to make our escape. Out the door we went and, as we jumped from the back porch, we abandoned our weapons to lighten our loads. We ran like two scared rabbits to the orchard and hid in the weeds where we could watch the house and listen for what happened next.

I was mad at Ike for bungling our only chance to end Edra's suffering, and as I crouched down in the weeds, breathing deeply to regain my breath after the harrowing ordeal and my swift retreat, I tried to figure out what to do next. "What in the hell can we do now? Especially if Floyd keeps knockin' her around?"

Ike moved close to me and sat back on his heels, with his knees on the ground. "I don't know," he said. "That darned wire! I would'a got him if it hadn't have been for that damned wire gettin' in my way!"

I didn't speak. I felt saddened and helpless in my failure to save my mother, and in the fact that I had abandoned her in her helplessness and her time of need. But it was only a couple of minutes after this when everyone except Floyd came through the back door, so it seemed to be over. It was over for everyone except Ike and me, anyway, for we were sure that as soon as Floyd caught us, we were dead.

I can only attribute what happened to divine intervention, preventing me and Ike from having our father's blood on our hands. If not for that wire, there was no way that Ike would have missed hitting Floyd with the pipe. And if not for Ike's actions preempting my own, there was no way that I would have missed when I threw that brick. One of us would surely have killed Floyd.

The consequences of our actions could have been horrendous, but we were both so young, we didn't really even begin to understand the seriousness of the situation. When I thought about that day in the years that followed, I could only thank God that a real tragedy was averted. I felt sure that Ike felt the same way, but my brother and I never talked about the incident after that day.

Floyd never said anything about what caused the wire to fall on that fateful day so we never knew whether he was aware of what had really happened. He had been so drunk at that time, he may have thought he had torn the wire down himself or that it was stretched too tight and had come loose on its own. Then again, the fact that he never hit Edra again after that day may indicate that he knew perfectly well what had actually occurred.

Ike and I were compadres who shared this traumatic event that formed an unbreakable bond between us. In the weeks following the incident, we ranged in the shadows, playing a game of cat and mouse, with the intention of avoiding Floyd foremost in our minds. Whenever it was time for Floyd to arrive home from work, Ike and I would go out to the edge of the field by the garden and hide in the tall weeds, and we would stay there until after dark. Once Floyd had gone to bed, Edra would come down the trail at the edge of the field, calling for us. I would usually linger there after Ike headed back toward the house. And I would hear my mother softly calling to me "Come home, Freddy Ray!"

Edra continued to keep us apprised of Floyd's location and activities with silent expressions and signals until time dulled the events of that terrible day.

After Ike and I made our move, Floyd and I became like strangers, even though we were living in the same house and it was then that I began to think of my youth as a childhood interrupted. I underwent a change because of this incident—a change that had been coming in stages and confounding me for a long, long time. I was never really a child again after that and yet in many ways, I would remain a child.

I would become haunted by vivid memories of my mother being beaten and her bruised face afterwards. Many times when I thought of Edra, I would be reminded of the incident.

* * *

While Edra was pregnant with me in 1945, an incident occurred that nearly overwhelmed me when I learned about it many years later. For reasons unknown, Floyd attacked Edra, kicking her in her rear end. John R., who was fourteen years old at the time and already bigger than Floyd, intervened when he saw what was happening. When John R. demanded that Floyd stop kicking Edra, Floyd picked up a baseball bat leaning against a nearby wall and began chasing John R., threatening to knock him in the head. It was a scary time for John R., but it momentarily stopped the abuse of Edra as Floyd chased John R., who easily outran him.

For a long time after that incident, John R. avoided Floyd as much as possible, just as Ike and I did after we interrupted Floyd as he was beating our mother.

* * *

For a long time after Ike and I made the attempt on Floyd's life, I seemed to range in the shadows, somewhere between being a boy and a man. In time, the memory of that day faded somewhat, but it would not completely leave me, for it was my constant companion, and I could not and would not separate myself from it. The ramifications of clinging to this memory would be manifested in many ways in the years to come and influence my life in phases and stages that would both confuse and aggravate my family and friends.

When I reached thirteen years of age, I more or less became a kid who was on his own, and I basically answered to no one. At the age of fourteen, I started walking or hitch-hiking the five miles to Haile each weekend, where I would drink beer and smoke with the older boys. On Christmas Eve when I was fourteen, I drank a pint of briar patch whiskey bought for two dollars from a local man. (Moonshine whiskey was sometimes called "briar patch whiskey" in our area.) When my older friends dumped me off at our front gate, I was drunk, dirty, and disheveled after getting drunk and falling across a small bonfire in Haile and being quickly rolled out of the fire and into the dust by a quick-thinking friend.

Elizabeth was at home for Christmas, huddled with my mother and grandmother around a space heater as I walked into the house that night. Needless to say, they were horrified by the sight I presented. They scolded me for being such a mess, saying, "Look at you! What a disgusting sight you are! You've been out running around with a bunch of roughnecks, and you are way too young to be doing that! What in the world is wrong with you?"

I barely remember them putting me to bed that night, but I recall quite clearly that I woke up the next morning with my head in dried vomit. That was one of the first samplings of the disastrous results I would achieve by trying to raise myself, a task I never did master.

* * *

It was long after dark and Ike had slipped back into the house. I lay shivering in the tall weeds at the edge of the field. I could hear Edra calling out to me, a soft call not much louder than a whisper, as she eased through the darkness in the field, "Come home, Freddy Ray!"

My body seemed to be gently rocking back and forth to fight the night's chill. Gradually I became aware of someone's hand on my shoulder. As I awakened, I realized that I must have fallen asleep in the car sometime before daybreak and been dreaming about the incident.

I opened my eyes and the first thing I saw was the sparkle of the dew on the Spanish moss hanging from the trees along the river's edge as the early morning sun peeped through the branches. I looked around and there was Diane, standing at the open door of the car, her hand on my shoulder, whispering softly, "Come home, Freddy Ray."

Afterword

Floyd Kinsolving Franklin was a man I never really knew very well at all, and I spent decades struggling with the mystery of our relationship. The fact that we did not have much of a father-son relationship bothered me for a long time, and I thought about it a lot after I married and had children of my own. For so many years, it was this powerful thing inside me that I could feel but not see, and I wrestled with it until I found a way to get it out into the open.

I decided to try to sort it all out in my mind, and I think that may have been the reason I was a loner who spent a lot of time in backwoods bars. I finally realized that I was depriving my own family of my time, and I needed to write my story in order to put it all behind me, relieve myself of the burden, get on with the life I created for myself, and be the husband and father that I should be.

When Floyd died in 1972, his death drove me to complete my search for answers to those questions that had passed through my mind for many years as if they were on an endless circular track that brought them by, it seemed, at regular intervals, with no chance of them being derailed or stopped, until the answers were matched up with them one by one and they were relegated to the past.

I couldn't help but feel that understanding the tragedy of Ervin Laird's death was the key to understanding my father. But it wasn't easy to piece together the story concerning the events that culminated in the 1933 killing. The afternoon I spent with Bo Pardue had resulted in a basic knowledge of the killing and what led up to it, but I still knew very little about that tragic event.

The killing occurred years before my birth and if it weren't for court records and eyewitness accounts, it might have remained an unfinished puzzle.

The urge to delve into the past for my peace of mind in the future was so great that I ignored the inevitable pain that such an excavation would entail, and jumped headfirst into the task of piecing it all together. I decided I would persevere until I had researched and thought it through completely. It was forty years after the tragedy before I finally found answers to the questions I had so often mulled over in my mind, and began to come to grips with the story and have a better understanding of both my father and myself.

I finally took the initiative to get Diane to search through court records. Given that the parish courthouse was only a block from where she worked, she had ample access to the records, and was able to conduct repeated searches in her spare time. I kept telling myself, *This is something I am doing for myself.* But as I got more involved, I began to feel as if there may be a message somewhere in the story—a message of some value to a parent who is letting valuable signals from their children go unnoticed. When children ask questions and seek their parents' love, it should be normal for that parental love to be demonstrated and expressed in the form of protection, companionship, and teaching during the formative years.

I have seen too many parents who were gruff and insensitive to their children when they asked a lot of questions, and I have never understood that. I looked up to Floyd when I was really young, watching him and working with him when I could, so I could learn to do some of the things he did when he was working. My need to learn continues to this day, because I love to be able to do whatever it takes to keep a household and a small farm going. I have learned to be a plumber, electrician, painter, carpenter, mechanic, equipment operator, and welder, among other things, simply by watching others and asking questions, or by doing things myself and learning by trial and error.

Initially, Diane's searches through the court records failed to turn up what I wanted—the record of my father's trial. I made a mental note to get Diane to try one more time to find Floyd's trial record. This time, she would be successful in her search and it would reveal that Arthur "Bo" Pardue's story was one that had to be sorted through carefully, for Bo's own father and an uncle signed affidavits placed into the trial records stating that Bo's reputation for truth and veracity in the community was bad. When I saw the affidavits in the trial record, and read what Bo's father had said about his son's reputation, I visited Uncle Walter and got his version of the story.

From what little I know of my father, he had a pretty rough childhood, himself. And then when he was twenty-eight years old, he loaded on himself a heavy weight in the taking of another man's life. That weight he carried for so long was transferred to me in a sense when I undertook the researching and telling of this story. And I felt that I could now lay it down for both of us, forever.

For the years that my father and I had kept each other at a distance, never talking to one another except as if we were almost strangers, I felt now as if I could forgive and be forgiven. It seems symbolic that I myself had reached the age of twenty-eight years before I began the process of unloading the final burden—a process which would lead me to forgiving my father. That process of forgiveness began in 1973 while I was reliving my past as I spent the night in my car overlooking the Ouachita River. Floyd became a Christian a couple of years after

Ike and I made the attempt on his life, so I know that he was forgiven for his misdeeds by God.

In the process of sorting everything out, I matured a great deal, but I felt I needed to write my story in order to complete my transformation. In telling this story, I have come full circle and my story is complete. After completing the first draft, I realized I had no more ill feelings and few regrets.

I regret that I never got a chance to tell my mother and grandmother how much they meant to me. In 1968, Edra died much too soon, from a heart attack that had been brought on by too many years of hard work and too much worry for a person so precious. I wish I could tell her that I have reached this point in my life and resolved the inner conflicts I had battled for so long.

I also regret that I never got to make meaningful peace with my father while he was still alive. But I feel that peace has somehow been found for the soul of Floyd Franklin, and peace has also been found for mine. At this point in my life, I feel more blessed than I deserve to be, and I am a happy man.

And considering that our family had no major catastrophes or tragedies, I guess it's true what they say: *all is well that ends well.*

Acknowledgments

First of all, I want to thank God for bringing me to this point in my life where I know peace and I know where I am going. No longer am I the reckless, wandering and lost soul I was in my youth.

I would like to thank my family and the many friends who encouraged me through the years as I worked on construction projects throughout much of the United States and worked on this story in my spare time.

A very special thanks goes to my wife, Diane, for her assistance with my research, and for always believing in me during this process.

The completion of this book would not have been possible without the invaluable input of Vivien Kooper, whose editing smoothed out the rough edges and helped to clarify what I was trying to say.

CPSIA information can be obtained at www.ICGtesting.com
Printed in the USA
BVOW08s1718290415

398279BV00007B/369/P